RAND NATIONAL DEFENSE RESEARCH INSTITUTE

What Works Best When Building Partner Capacity and Under What Circumstances?

Christopher Paul, Colin P. Clarke, Beth Grill, Stephanie Young, Jennifer D. P. Moroney, Joe Hogler, Christine Leah

Prepared for the Office of the Secretary of Defense

The research described in this report was prepared for the Office of the Secretary of Defense (OSD). The research was conducted within the RAND National Defense Research Institute, a federally funded research and development center sponsored by OSD, the Joint Staff, the Unified Combatant Commands, the Navy, the Marine Corps, the defense agencies, and the defense Intelligence Community under Contract W74V8H-06-C-0002.

Library of Congress Cataloging-in-Publication Data is available for this publication.
ISBN: 978-0-8330-7850-6

Cover photo: Army Major Tony Miller of the Tennessee National Guard explains shipping labels on outbound cargo during a training event. Africa Deployment Assistance Partnership Teams traveled to Uganda from February 20 to February 24, 2012, to train Ugandan soldiers in logistics requirements for deployments. American Forces Press Service courtesy photo (www.defense.gov).

Published 2013 by the RAND Corporation
1776 Main Street, P.O. Box 2138, Santa Monica, CA 90407-2138
1200 South Hayes Street, Arlington, VA 22202-5050
4570 Fifth Avenue, Suite 600, Pittsburgh, PA 15213-2665
RAND URL: http://www.rand.org/
To order RAND documents or to obtain additional information, contact
Distribution Services: Telephone: (310) 451-7002;
Fax: (310) 451-6915; Email: order@rand.org

Preface

Working with allies and partner countries to build their defense capacity, ensure access for contingent operations, and strengthen relationships with their military and security forces is an important U.S. military undertaking. This undertaking can include a tremendous range of activities, from the obvious and visible, such as training, equipping, and exercising with partner forces, to the less conspicuous, such as holding bilateral talks, conducting workshops and conferences, and providing education.

It is often challenging to determine whether and in what combination these activities have contributed to U.S. objectives. The challenge stems from both the difficulty of measuring the activities themselves (the inputs and the outputs) and the difficulty of determining their impact on multiple U.S. objectives.

This research uses detailed historical case studies, analyzed individually and collectively, to provide a foundation of evidence for future resource allocation and policymaking in the specific security cooperation area of building partner capacity. The findings should be of interest to policymakers and stakeholders in the broader security cooperation arena in the Office of the Secretary of Defense, the regional Combatant Commands (and the related service components), and the U.S. Department of State.

This is a summary of a larger, controlled-access companion report of the same title. That report is available to those with a need to know and appropriate clearances.

This research was sponsored jointly by the Office of Cost Assessment and Program Evaluation in the Office of the Secretary of Defense and the Office of the Under Secretary of Defense for Policy and was conducted within the International Security and Defense Policy Center of the RAND National Defense Research Institute, a federally funded research and development center sponsored by the Office of the Secretary of Defense, the Joint Staff, the Unified Combatant Commands, the Navy, the Marine Corps, the defense agencies, and the defense Intelligence Community.

For more information on the International Security and Defense Policy Center, see http://www.rand.org/nsrd/ndri/centers/isdp.html or contact the director (contact information is provided on the web page).

Contents

Figures

Tables

Boxes

Summary

Purpose of This Research

The United States has a long history of helping other nations develop and improve their military and other security forces. U.S. Department of Defense (DoD) efforts with a goal of building partner capacity (BPC) continue in earnest in the contemporary era and will remain prominent defense activities in the future. However, changing economic realities and the ongoing reductions in overall defense spending related to the end of more than a decade of war will affect the funding available for these initiatives. How can DoD increase the effectiveness of its efforts to build partner capacity while also increasing the efficiency of those efforts? *What can the history of U.S. BPC efforts tell us about which approaches to capacity building are likely to be more or less effective under different circumstances?*[1] Answering this question is the principal ambition of this report. The goal is not only to provide satisfactory answers about correlates of effectiveness but to do so from a firm base of evidence.

---

1 Note that this report addresses only the effectiveness of the approaches in terms of BPC outcomes. Although many of the factors related to effectiveness also have implications for efficiency, we do not address that topic here, and it remains an important area for future research.

Data and Evidence

This report considers and compares historical case studies of U.S. efforts to build partner capacity in order to generate a base of evidence to inform policy discussions and investment decisions. We compare the results of U.S. BPC efforts since the end of the Cold War for 29 selected partner nations (PNs).[2] By examining 20 years of data on 29 systematically selected countries, we were able to build a solid foundation of evidence on the effectiveness of different features of capacity-building efforts under different conditions and in different contexts.

Each country case is divided into between two and four chronological phases. These phases served as the unit of analysis for the study. The average length of a phase is eight years, though some are shorter or longer. The length of each phase was determined holistically at the discretion of the individual case analyst. Phase changes do not reflect small-scale changes or changes on a single factor; rather, they indicate significant shifts and events affecting many factors (or perhaps a smaller number of particularly important factors) in the overall case. Each case also includes a baseline phase, from which we derived baseline outcome data. Taken together, the "actual" data phases, the null phases (in which no capacity building occurred), and the baseline phases total 100.

Each of these 100 phases represents a row in the project database. For each non-baseline phase, the data rows include scores for roughly 75 factors or variables.

Of the 100 phases, 38 are null or baseline phases, and 62 are "real" numbered phases in which the United States conducted BPC activities with discernable intent. In 55 of those 62 phases, at least one of the primary objectives was a form of capacity building—that is, relationship building or securing access was not the only primary objective, and efforts included some kind of earnest attempt to build

---

[2] To protect the sensitivity of some details of the partnerships, this report does not list the 29 selected partners. However, we do rely on examples drawn from the less sensitive of the 29 cases, as well as examples of other partnerships with which the authors are familiar. The full case studies are available in the controlled-access companion report.

actual capacity. (In the other seven phases, relationship building or access was the only discernible objective).[3] These 55 phases in which capacity building was a goal, then, constituted the analytic core of our analysis, which sought to discern the effectiveness—in different contexts—of different BPC efforts in actually building capacity. A total of 22 phases have relationship building or access as a primary objective; this set includes the seven phases noted previously, in which relationship building or access is the only objective, as well as 15 phases in which some sort of capacity building is a primary objective but relationship building or access is also a primary objective. Considering the 55 phases in which capacity building is an objective and removing phases in which relationship building or access is *also* a primary objective leaves a data subset of 40. These 40 phases represent "pure" efforts to build capacity. Most analyses in this report rely on either the $n = 55$ or the $n = 40$ subsets. Figure S.1 presents a Venn diagram of the various subsets of phases.

For each phase, we identified a set of *inputs* within a certain *context* that produced certain *outcomes*.[4] Patterns of these input, contextual, and outcome factors constitute evidence in the study. For each phase of each case, we measured approximately 75 different input, contextual, or outcome factors.

3 Although it may seem tautological to have to ask whether or not the BPC objectives in our case studies actually involved capacity building, it is not. We recognize that U.S. BPC activities are employed in pursuit of a variety of foreign policy and national security objectives. Usually, at least one of those objectives is some sort of increase in a partner's defense capacity; sometimes, however, BPC tools and funds are offered in pursuit of a different objective, such as persuading a partner to allow access by U.S. forces (e.g., basing rights, overflight rights, land transit rights) or otherwise improving the relationship between the partner and the United States in pursuit of a foreign policy benefit *without actually building any capacity.*

4 Input factors include BPC expenditures, activities, and contributions made by the United States, the partner country, or other partners, along with any relevant details of those activities. Context factors describe the environment (writ large) in which BPC activities are conducted and can include features of the partner nation (e.g., the strength of its economy, its baseline defense capability) or characteristics of its neighbors or region (e.g., level of regional security threats, correspondence between partner goals and U.S. goals). Outcome factors describe the results of BPC activities in the described contexts; in these cases, the outcomes of interest concern whether or not capacity was built and how much.

Figure S.1
Venn Diagram of the Subsets of Phases in the Data

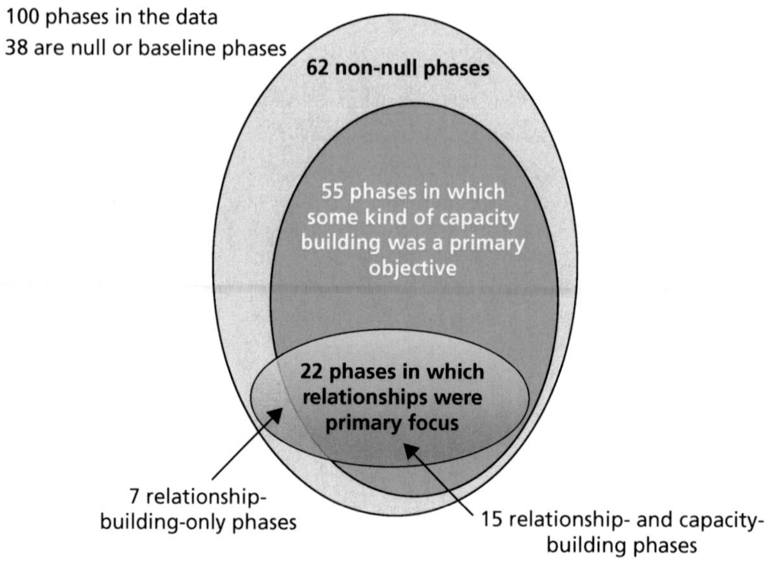

RAND *MG1253/1-S.1*

Each case includes a detailed narrative and a host of factors scored across the different phases, supporting two types of analyses: single-case lessons learned with discursive examples and comparative or aggregate analysis across phases and cases.

This evidence either supports or fails to support a collection of hypotheses, with each hypothesis represented by one or more factors.

Findings

Most of the project hypotheses are based on received wisdom on BPC effectiveness, drawn either from other scholarly sources or from conversations with BPC stakeholders and practitioners. As such, most of these hypotheses received empirical support from the comparative evidence gathered for this study. What varies, however, is the strength of the correlations observed and, thus, the strength of support offered by the evidence. The following key findings are based on our analysis.

Matching matters: BPC is most effective when U.S. objectives align with PN objectives and when BPC efforts align with the partner's baseline capabilities and absorptive capacity.

This single prominent observation inspired the central metaphor of this report: find the right ladder, find the right rung. The historical cases show that BPC is effective when the capacity being built meets the interests of both the partner country and the United States (the right ladder) and when the BPC activities are a good match for the partner's baseline capability in that area and its capacity to absorb new materiel, training, and so on (the right rung).

Context matters: Certain characteristics or features of PNs make BPC more likely to be effective.

Specifically, the following properties are associated with greater effectiveness in BPC, historically:

- PN invests its own funds to support or sustain capacity
- PN has sufficient absorptive capacity
- PN has high governance indicators
- PN has a strong economy
- PN shares security interests with the United States.

Independent of PN context, there are several factors wholly under the control of the United States that correlate strongly with BPC effectiveness.

These factors, which are strongly endorsed by our analyses, are as follows:

- spending more money on BPC or undertaking more BPC initiatives
- consistency in both the funding and implementation of these initiatives
- matching BPC efforts with PN objectives and absorptive capacity
- including a sustainment component in the initiatives.

BPC is complex, but we found that there are some clear best practices for those conducting BPC, clear best traits for desirable partners, and clear best practices for recipient partners. The results demonstrate that when all three have been followed, effectiveness has ensued. *That is, if BPC is consistently funded and delivered, supported and sustained, well matched to partner capabilities and interests, and shared with a partner that supports the effort and is healthy economically and in terms of governance, prospects for effective BPC are very good.* The results also suggest that BPC can still be effective when only some practices are followed or when only some conditions are met. BPC done well, done consistently, and matched to partner absorptive capacities and interests can be effective even when the partner is not particularly robust in any dimension at the outset.

The strongest and most consistent correlations, however, are for factors at the seam of U.S. and PN control: factors related to the alignment of interests and the matching of capacity-building activities to PN objectives and to the ability of the PN to absorb and retain the materiel and training provided.

The criticality of these seam or matching factors inspired the overriding metaphor for the study, "find the right ladder, find the right rung."

Recommendations

The study findings suggest several clear recommendations for DoD both in the future planning and execution of BPC and in investing in the creation and maintenance of BPC capabilities.

Where possible, choose partners that have or can adopt the attributes, characteristics, or behaviors that are associated with effective BPC.

We recognize that, sometimes, foreign policy imperatives or the nature or location of a threat dictate or force priorities when choosing partner nations. However, when there is flexibility in partners and priorities, choose partners that have or will adopt contextual factors associated with BPC effectiveness. Specifically, when all else is equal, give preference to countries

- that are willing to invest their own funds to support or sustain capacity
- that have sufficient absorptive capacity
- that have high governance indicators
- that have strong and healthy economies
- whose broad strategic interests predominantly align with U.S. interests in the region.

Regardless of the partner or context, choose BPC goals and activities to correspond with what the partner wants or needs and what it is capable of absorbing.

As noted, strategic imperatives can compel partnerships in which the partner lacks some of the attributes that were prioritized in the first recommendation. Whether working with ideal partners or suboptimal partners, prospects for effective BPC increase dramatically when specific BPC objectives align with specific partner interests (independent of broader alignment with U.S. interests) and when the specific BPC activities conducted are well matched to partner baseline capabilities and absorptive capacity. Find the right ladder, find the right rung!

For continued BPC effectiveness, the United States should build or maintain partner capabilities in the following ways.

- *Plan BPC activities to match both U.S. and PN needs and objectives.* Finding the intersection between U.S. and PN objectives is easy in some instances and quite tricky in others—especially when the intersection of interests is limited or nuanced. Planning and coordinating BPC activities to meet U.S. and PN objectives (and thus maximize prospects for success, both in BPC and in broader policy) is nontrivial. Such capabilities are and remain essential.
- *Identify baseline PN absorptive capacity and match BPC activities to what the partner can absorb.* Matching activities to PN baseline capabilities and absorptive capacity is also critical. DoD must

have the capability to conduct needs assessments, identify baseline partner capabilities, and determine PN forces' initial levels of absorptive capacity (including equipment, organizational characteristics, readiness, the extent of existing training, technological sophistication, education, language abilities, and doctrine) to be able to optimally plan and match BPC activities to PN needs.

- *Build ministerial capacity and otherwise develop absorptive capacity.* Ministerial capacity (the capability of a partner's ministry of defense or ministry of interior to plan for and manage the partner's military and security forces) is foundational for other forms of capacity. Further, we found that ministerial capacity can be improved even when PN absorptive capacity is generally low and that ministerial capacity building can, itself, improve a partner's absorptive capacity even when baseline absorptive capacity is low. Such increases could enable future capacity building in other areas. These capabilities should be central to the future BPC toolbox.
- *Consider sustainment capabilities in BPC planning.* Sustainment considerations are highly correlated with long-term effectiveness in the 29 cases discussed here. Whether it involves building a separate logistics capability or funding stream or expanding existing programs and capabilities to facilitate sustainment, effective BPC requires sustainment.

Acknowledgments

First and foremost, we owe a debt of gratitude to our thoughtful and engaged sponsor points of contact, David Lowe in the Office of Cost Assessment and Program Evaluation in the Office of the Secretary of Defense (OSD/CAPE) and Maureen Bannon in the Office of the Under Secretary of Defense for Policy (OUSD[P]). Their guidance and support was instrumental in the development of this report. We are also indebted to several other DoD personnel who participated in interim briefings, commented on draft slides, or otherwise provided valuable feedback on the research: Timothy Bright, Tom Johnson, and Melissa Kirkner of OSD/CAPE; Aaron Jay of OUSD(P); James Miner of the Defense Security Cooperation Agency; and CAPT Connie Frizzell, CAPT John Sniegowski, and CDR John Mann of the Joint Staff (J5).

We thank several of our RAND colleagues who offered engaging discussion on this topic, foundational insights, or comments on draft materials: Terrence Kelly, Thomas Szayna, Michael McNerney, Seth Jones, James Dobbins, Michael McGee, and Jessica Yeats. RAND administrative assistant Maria Falvo, editor Lauren Skrabala, and production editor Jocelyn Lofstrom contributed substantially to the form and fettle of the final product, as did the two scholars who reviewed this document as part of the RAND quality assurance process: RAND's Jefferson Marquis and Professor Sean McFate of National Defense University.

Finally, we thank all the desk officers, action officers, and other subject-matter experts in OSD, at the combatant commands, in the components, and elsewhere who took the time to share information and insights about BPC in the specific country cases. We refrain from thanking you all by name to keep the terms of our anonymous interviews, but you know who you are, and we appreciate your contributions.

Any errors or omissions remain the responsibility of the authors alone.

Abbreviations

BPC	building partner capacity
COCOM	combatant command
CoESPU	Center of Excellence for Stability Police Units
DCS	Direct Commercial Sales
DoD	U.S. Department of Defense
DoS	U.S. Department of State
DSART	Defense Sector Assessment Rating Tool
DSCA	Defense Security Cooperation Agency
FMF	Foreign Military Financing
FMS	Foreign Military Sales
FY	fiscal year
GDP	gross domestic product
GEF	*Guidance for Employment of the Force*
IMET	International Military Education and Training
NADR	Nonproliferation, Antiterrorism, Demining, and Related Programs

OEF-P	Operation Enduring Freedom–Philippines
OSD	Office of the Secretary of Defense
OSD/CAPE	Office of Cost Assessment and Program Evaluation, Office of the Secretary of Defense
OUSD(P)	Office of the Under Secretary of Defense for Policy
PN	partner nation
QCA	qualitative comparative analysis
USAFRICOM	U.S. Africa Command
USAID	U.S. Agency for International Development
USCENTCOM	U.S. Central Command
USEUCOM	U.S. European Command
USPACOM	U.S. Pacific Command
USSOUTHCOM	U.S. Southern Command
WIF	Warsaw Initiative Fund

CHAPTER ONE

Introduction: Find the Right Ladder, Find the Right Rung

Purpose of This Study and Central Questions

The United States has a long history of helping other nations develop and improve their military and other security forces. U.S. Department of Defense (DoD) efforts with a goal of building partner capacity (BPC) continue in earnest in the contemporary era and will remain prominent defense activities in the future. However, changing economic realities and the ongoing reductions in overall defense spending related to the end of more than a decade of war will affect the funding available for these initiatives. How can DoD increase the effectiveness of its efforts to build partner capacity while also increasing the efficiency of those efforts? *What can the history of U.S. BPC efforts tell us about which approaches are likely to be more or less effective under different circumstances?* Answering these questions is the principal ambition of this report.[1]

This report considers and compares historical case studies of U.S. efforts to build partner capacity in order to generate a base of evidence to inform policy discussions and investment decisions. We compare the results of U.S. BPC efforts since the end of the Cold War for 29 selected partner nations (PNs). By examining 20 years of data on 29 systematically selected countries, we were able to build a solid foun-

[1] Note that this report addresses only the effectiveness of the approaches in terms of BPC outcomes. While many of the factors related to effectiveness also have implications for efficiency, we do not address that topic here, and it remains an important area for future research.

dation of evidence on the effectiveness of different features of capacity-building efforts under different conditions and in different contexts.

The Logic of the Inquiry

Working with allies and partners to build their defense capacity, ensure access for contingent operations, and strengthen relationships with their military and security forces is an important U.S. military undertaking. This undertaking can include a tremendous range of activities, from the obvious and visible, such as training, equipping, and exercising with partner forces, to the less conspicuous, such as holding bilateral talks, conducting workshops and conferences, and providing education.

It is often challenging to determine whether and in what combination these activities have contributed to U.S. objectives. The challenge stems from both the difficulty of measuring the activities themselves (the inputs and the outputs) and the difficulty of determining their impact on multiple U.S. objectives.

This report uses detailed historical narratives for 20-year spans in 29 countries to identify the features and characteristics of effective approaches to BPC, as well as the conditions and contextual factors that improve or inhibit effectiveness. While each case retains its own distinct narrative, we evaluate certain features (and the BPC activities undertaken in each case) consistently across cases. For each phase of each case, we sought to identify a set of inputs, a set of conditions or contextual factors, and a set of resulting outcomes.[2] This method

[2] Input factors include BPC expenditures, activities, and contributions made by the United States, the partner country, or other partners, along with any relevant details of those activities. Context factors describe the environment (writ large) in which BPC activities are conducted and can include features of the partner nation (e.g., the strength of its economy, its baseline defense capability) or characteristics of its neighbors or region (e.g., level of regional security threats, correspondence between partner goals and U.S. goals). Outcome factors describe the results of BPC activities in the described contexts; in these cases, the outcomes of interest concern whether or not capacity was built and how much.

produced two kinds of data: the detailed case-study narratives and a substantial cross-case comparative data set.

We use these two kinds of data to test a number of hypotheses about effective practices for or features of BPC, or about conditions or contextual factors that influence capacity building. These project hypotheses are listed in Chapter Three. They include "received wisdom" about BPC (what we think we know from common sense and anecdotal experience but lack a good evidentiary foundation for), hypotheses offered or requested by our sponsors in the Office of the Secretary of Defense (OSD), and hypotheses developed inductively during the preliminary case-study investigations. We use four "parent" hypotheses to categorize the various project hypotheses:

1. The way in which the United States plans, resources, and executes BPC influences effectiveness.
2. You can lead a horse to water but you cannot make it drink: Low partner motivation is adverse to capacity outcomes.
3. PN baseline capabilities (in government, economy, and defense) influence the effectiveness of BPC.
4. The broader context of a case (the geopolitical situation, other neighbors and partners) influences the effectiveness of BPC.

Preview of Results

The results, presented in Chapter Five, identify a variety of practices or contextual factors that are correlated with success in BPC, some under the control of the United States as the contributor of assistance and some that are either under PN control or intrinsic characteristics. The strongest and most consistent correlations, however, are for factors at the seam of U.S. and PN control: factors related to the alignment of interests and the matching of capacity-building activities to PN objectives and to the ability of the PN to absorb and retain the materiel and training provided.

The criticality of these seam or matching factors inspired the title of this chapter and the overriding metaphor for the study, "find the right ladder, find the right rung." Effective U.S. BPC efforts in the 29 cases mentioned here almost always address capability areas that are central to both U.S. and PN interests (the right ladder) and build on existing baseline PN capabilities, without providing more sophisticated equipment, assistance, or training than PN forces are able to absorb (the right rung). When both the U.S. and PN leadership have been enthusiastic about developing and improving capabilities, and when assistance has been well matched to the PN's context and baseline capabilities, success has followed.

Finally, holistic analyses of the 29 case narratives led to three additional key results.

First, *relationships matter.* When the primary objective of BPC engagement is more about building a relationship or securing access (instead of actually building capacity), capacity building is often less effective. This is neither surprising nor problematic; if BPC activities can be used to realize important foreign policy objectives, then that is a successful use of BPC resources. It does not necessarily have to lead to success in building capacity.

Relationships matter in other aspects of BPC, too. Even when relationship building or access is not a primary objective of a BPC initiative, there is a strong correlation between effectiveness in building capacity and good or improving relationships between the United State and the PN. The narratives suggest that this correlation flows in both directions and feeds back in both directions, with better relations making capacity building more effective and demonstrations of effectiveness in capacity building improving relations.

Second, *BPC takes time.* In many cases, progress substantially lagged investment, not only because execution takes time, but also because of false starts, delays, or time consumed in establishing processes and routinizing interactions. In many cases, significant groundwork needed to be done before any actual capacity could be built. This included in some cases of establishing and building trust and relationships with the PN and PN forces; and in other cases, it involved building partner absorptive capacity (so, building the capacity to have capacity built).

Third, *9/11 was a watershed in U.S. BPC*. While DoD activities prior to September 11, 2001, included BPC, pre-9/11 efforts were less robust, less focused, less well funded, and overall less effective. After 9/11, many BPC relationships switched emphases, received greater funding, and were made more robust, with specific goals in mind. These efforts were, on the whole, more effective than the efforts of the previous decade.

The Organization of This Report

The remainder of this report explains the study's approach and presents the findings from our analyses in five chapters and an appendix. Chapter Two provides background and context, describing the type and character of U.S. BPC efforts, defining key terminology, giving examples of different BPC objectives, and, most importantly, describing the tool used to assess BPC outcomes, the modified Defense Sector Assessment Rating Tool (DSART). Chapter Three clearly lays out the project hypotheses and describes the factors that represented those hypotheses in the study analyses. Chapter Four explains the process by which we selected the 29 cases studied. Chapter Five presents the data analyses and results, including some methodological detail and tests of the hypotheses described in Chapter Three. Chapter Six concludes the report by exploring the implications of the study's results and making recommendations. The body of the report is supported by an appendix containing details on the elements used in scoring BPC outcomes.

To protect the sensitivity of some details of the partnerships, this report does not list the 29 selected partners. However, we do rely on examples drawn from the less sensitive of the 29 cases, as well as examples of other partnerships with which the authors are familiar. As noted in the preface, this report is a condensed version of a larger, controlled-access companion report on the same topic. That companion volume includes an expanded version of Chapter Four, some additional examples throughout, and an additional (and quite substantial) appendix containing a case narrative for each of the 29 selected cases.

CHAPTER TWO

U.S. Department of Defense Efforts to Build Partner Capacity

This chapter provides background on U.S. BPC efforts, along with key terminology and information about authorities and various approaches to working with PNs in a BPC context. It begins with an overview of BPC, describing important terms and the basic oversight of BPC efforts. Next, the chapter continues with a discussion of how BPC objectives are identified and pursued—in other words, the BPC process. We focus, in particular, on how the study drew on an important assessment tool, the DSART, as a way to methodically evaluate the effectiveness of historical cases of BPC. Finally, the chapter concludes with a selection of examples that highlight the way in which BPC objectives and activities ultimately translate to partner capabilities. These examples introduce and illustrate some of the conditions and complexities under which the case studies described later in the report were undertaken.

Key Terminology

Security cooperation and *security assistance* are terms with a long history of usage. According to the Defense Security Cooperation Agency (DSCA) website, security cooperation includes "those activities conducted with allies and friendly nations to: build relationships that promote specified U.S. interests, build allied and friendly nation capabilities for self-defense and coalition operations, [and] provide U.S. forces with peacetime and contingency access."[1]

Security assistance consists of "a group of programs, authorized by law, through which the U.S. Department of Defense (DoD) or commercial contractors provide defense articles and services in support of national policies and objectives."[2] The U.S. strategy for security assistance is set forth as a multiyear plan developed by the U.S. Department of State (DoS) and coordinated with key elements of DoD. DoS also administers security assistance efforts in close coordination with DoD, which (generally) executes them. Because the goals of security assistance efforts must be in concert with the assistance goals of DoD, and because DoD has a vested interest in the nature and outcome of such efforts, DoD correctly views it as a subset of its overall security cooperation efforts.[3] Examples of these programs include Foreign Military Sales (FMS), Foreign Military Financing (FMF), International Military Education and Training (IMET), and Direct Commercial Sales (DCS).

Building partner capacity, the key term used in this report, is a term of art employed to describe "targeted efforts to improve the collective capabilities and performance of the Department of Defense and its partners."[4] The term emerged at the height of Operations Enduring Freedom and Iraqi Freedom. Its debut in the security cooperation vernacular was intended to raise and focus the profile of specific security

---

[1] Defense Security Cooperation Agency, "Frequently Asked Questions (FAQs)," web page, last updated August 15, 2012.

[2] DCSA, 2012. For a full list of security assistance programs, see U.S. Department of Defense, *Security Assistance Management Manual (SAMM)*, Washington, D.C., DoD 5105.38-M, April 30, 2012.

[3] U.S. Code, Title 22, "Foreign Relations and Intercourse," Section 2305, "National Security Assistance Strategy."

[4] U.S. Department of Defense, *Building Partnership Capacity: QDR Execution Roadmap*, Washington, D.C., May 22, 2006b, para. 1.3.1. That report is an evolving document. It includes guidance on how DoD should train and equip foreign military forces and discusses the need to improve the capacity of other PN security services (e.g., stability police, border guards, customs). The concept also refers to the need to improve DoD's ability to work with nonmilitary forces (i.e., other U.S. government agencies, nongovernmental organizations, coalition partners, and the private sector) in an integrated operational context.

cooperation activities and to show their relevance to combating terrorism, in particular. DoD documents, such as the 2006 *Quadrennial Defense Review Report* and the 2006 *Building Partnership Capacity: QDR Execution Roadmap*, emphasized BPC as the effort to build the security and defense capabilities of partner countries, enabling them to make valuable contributions to coalition operations and to improve their own indigenous capabilities.[5] Although the term only dates back to roughly 2003, the concept is comfortably applicable across the appropriate range of security cooperation activities dating back to the end of the Cold War; the fact that the term was not in use at the beginning of our historical study period had no impact on our analyses.

Other terms are used to describe what we refer to as BPC. In the military services, OSD, the Joint Staff, and the combatant commands (COCOMs), a wide range of terminology has arisen, mostly to suit the varying needs of specific communities that are interested in working with partner militaries. Out of the morass of military assistance efforts in Iraq and Afghanistan, for example, comes the term *security force assistance*. Those charged with conducting such activities no doubt saw the need to account for the fact that the U.S. military in these countries was "building the capacity" of not just military forces but also national police and other nonmilitary security forces. Similarly, from the pages of the 2006 *Quadrennial Defense Review Report* came the terms *building partner capacity* and *building partnership capacity*. The relative vagueness of these two terms spawned the related term, *building partner relationships*, in an effort to clarify the difference between "partner" and "partnership." When we say "BPC," we are in no way trying to standardize the terminology; instead, we mean it in an inclusive way that captures all of these meanings, leaving the lexicographical debate to others.

Finally, it is important to distinguish between the various types of assistance that the United States provides to foreign partners. We have already mentioned the key role of DoS in administering security assistance; other agencies, while not quite so focused on military assistance,

---

[5] U.S. Department of Defense, *Quadrennial Defense Review Report*, Washington, D.C., February 6, 2006a; DoD, 2006b.

nonetheless contribute in this area. For example, the U.S. Agency for International Development (USAID), which is chiefly responsible for development assistance (i.e., economic growth, democracy and governance, medical assistance), also plays a role in what has become known collectively as "security-sector reform."[6] U.S. security-sector reform efforts draw on not only DoD security cooperation activities but also counternarcotics, stability and reconstruction, law enforcement, and other activities administered by USAID, the U.S. Drug Enforcement Agency, the Federal Bureau of Investigation, U.S. Customs and Border Protection, and others. Such collaboration and cooperation is essential to the efficient and effective implementation of U.S. assistance programs, but it does tend to blur the lines of responsibility. This report attempts to stay neatly inside the DoD "lane," but, as seen in many of the case studies, it is simply not possible (or wise) to always look at DoD efforts in isolation.

Several other key terms are used throughout this report, including *program*, *objective* or *purpose*, *activity*, *funding source*, and *initiative*. In the absence of official definitions for these terms, we offer working definitions based on (mostly) shared common usage.

Programs can be thought of as a set of activities designed and coordinated to achieve BPC objectives or purposes.[7] Programs can be thought of as a set of activities coordinated to achieve a certain set of objectives. Programs have the following defining characteristics, at a minimum:

- specific objectives or purposes
- activities
- authorities
- funding sources and other resources.

High-level *objectives* can originate from any combination of departmental, service-level, COCOM, or legislative sources and may

6 U.S. Agency for International Development, U.S. Department of Defense, and U.S. Department of State, *Security Sector Reform*, Washington, D.C., February 2009.

7 Programs are often used to conduct activities for multiple purposes.

be related to a country, a region, or even a global issue. DoD sources, such as the OSD's *Guidance for Employment of the Force* (GEF) and COCOM theater campaign plans, are designed to support national objectives and direct the U.S. military's overall planning effort, including that for BPC.

Supporting *objectives* or *purposes* are specific military or interagency mission areas, such as stabilization and reconstruction, peacekeeping, humanitarian assistance, and countering weapons of mass destruction, and are derived from and related to higher-level objectives. Understanding the objective and purpose helps the planner focus on the proper partners, capabilities, and resources required to meet an objective.

Activities, discussed in greater detail later in this chapter, are methods used by a particular program that are directed, funded, or supervised by program managers, such as training courses, workshops, exercises, and transfers of equipment or supplies to PNs. "Activities" are generic in this sense (for example, "combined exercises"), but they can become specific in the context of implementing a program or plan. An example of a specific activity designed to achieve program objectives include U.S. Southern Command's (USSOUTHCOM's) PANAMAX multinational exercise or U.S. Central Command's (USCENTCOM's) annual Regional Cooperation Exercise, an initiative to improve multilateral cooperation on counterterrorism and humanitarian crisis response in Central Asia.

Authorities are derived from legislative sources (i.e., public law, U.S. Code). In some cases, legislative authorities specifically establish a program and its purpose, describing who may use it and how it may be used. In many cases, however, these sources are less directive, giving the COCOM or service the flexibility to design programs under broad authority that permits engagement with foreign partners.[8] In other

---

8 Programs without specific legislative authorization are typically the result of commanders' projects that leverage existing authorities to work with PNs. Such non-programmed programs are usually implemented through an ad hoc collection of funding sources (for example, operations and maintenance budgets).

cases, DoD has limited or shared authority and must coordinate with other agencies to develop and implement programs.

Legal authorities to conduct security cooperation activities, set forth in Title 10 and Title 22 of the U.S. Code, establish the principal departmental divisions of labor between DoS and DoD. DoD plays a role in two general categories of security cooperation programs. The first category represents Title 10 programs that DoD manages and executes, such as the Defense Personnel Exchange Program and the Combating Terrorism Fellowship Program. The second category contains Title 22 programs overseen by DoS but executed by DoD. These programs include those under various parts of Title 22, Chapter 32, Subchapter II ("Military Assistance and Sales") of the U.S. Code, which addresses, for example, FMS and IMET.[9] Some, but not all, security cooperation programs have accompanying directives or operating instructions that specify the program's objectives, how resources are allotted and expended, and the various stakeholder responsibilities. Others do not. For example, multilateral conferences or workshops sponsored by DoD components are governed only by broad Title 10 U.S. Code guidance, specifically, 10 U.S.C. 1051 and 10 U.S.C. 168.[10]

Some security cooperation programs have included so-called dual-key legislative provisions that require the Secretary of State's concurrence on military training and equipping programs approved by DoD.[11]

Funding sources may be large umbrella resource streams that provide resources to a collection of programs (sometimes referred to as an "initiative") or to a specific program. The key difference between authorities and funding sources is simple: Authorities give permission for a commander to act, and funding sources enable that action.

---

[9] U.S. Code, Title 22, "Foreign Relations and Intercourse," Chapter 39, "Arms Export Control," Sections 2761, 2762, 2769, and 2763.

[10] U.S. Code, Title 10, "Armed Forces," Section 1051, "Multilateral, Bilateral, or Regional Cooperation Programs: Payment of Personnel Expenses"; U.S. Code, Title 10, "Armed Forces," Section 168, "Military-to-Military Contacts and Comparable Activities."

[11] Sharif Calfee, Joseph Lee, Peter Crandall, and Young Rock An, "Enhancing Interagency Cooperation," *Joint Force Quarterly*, No. 61, 2nd Quarter 2011.

An initiative is a program or a collection of related programs that draw on a funding source established to pursue a particular set of goals. An example of a program that feeds various initiatives is the Warsaw Initiative Fund (WIF), which funds a variety of programs and initiatives in Central and Southern Europe and Eurasia, including the Cooperative Threat Reduction Program.[12] Another example is the Nonproliferation, Antiterrorism, Demining, and Related Programs (NADR), which funds many security cooperation programs globally.[13]

Some programs are specifically authorized by legislation and, as such, may have a dedicated funding source.[14] Most programs, however, are funded by other, less narrow sources, such as operations and maintenance funds. Examples include exercises overseen by the Chairman of the Joint Chiefs of Staff, which are funded by the Joint Staff, and military-to-military contacts, which are often (but not always) funded by Traditional COCOM Activity authority. In each of these cases, DoD uses a specific authority to use its operations and maintenance funds for a given security cooperation activity. In some cases, these funds are then reimbursed, but more often than not, the security cooperation activity comes at the expense of another defense priority. Still other programs are funded by DoS, although they are executed by DoD, as described earlier.

Table 2.1 shows the relationship among the terms discussed here and provides brief examples.

---

[12] See U.S. Department of Defense Office of the Inspector General, *Joint Warfighting and Readiness: DoD Execution of the Warsaw Initiative Program*, Arlington, Va., D-2005-085, July 1, 2005. WIF also funds certain Air Force security cooperation activities, such as Regional Airspace Initiative studies that have been conducted in Eastern Europe.

[13] NADR also demonstrates how titles can cause confusion about what is a funding source and what is a program. Although the word "programs" is part of NADR's official name, it is actually a funding source that feeds those programs. For example, NADR provides funding for the DoS Export Control and Related Border Security program and Antiterrorism Assistance program, as well as the Small Arms/Light Weapons destruction program managed by DoD's Defense Threat Reduction Agency.

[14] These programs typically have a defined funding source in an appropriated budget that is tied to its authorization (such as the Afghanistan Security Forces Fund) and do not have to solicit funds from other sources to execute activities.

Table 2.1
Distinguishing the Terms

Term	Defining Characteristics	Example
Program	Specific mission/objectives, manager, activities, and reporting requirements	Civil-Military Emergency Preparedness Program
High-level objective	Originate from guidance or strategy; may relate to a country, region, or global issue	Facilitation of regional information sharing in emergency preparedness planning
Supporting objective/ purpose	Specific military or interagency mission area	Disaster relief
Activity	Specific kinds of interactions funded by programs that include U.S. and partner representatives; designed to address specific objectives	Workshop
Authorities	Set of rules that govern security cooperation programs and activities	10 U.S.C., 22 U.S.C.
Funding source	Money	WIF
Initiative	A program or set of programs drawing on the resources of a funding source established for such purposes	Regional Airspace Initiatives studies funded by WIF

Armed with this theoretical understanding, we turn next to how BPC is managed within DoD.

Setting Objectives for Building Partner Capacity

High-level objectives for BPC are typically derived from a variety of sources, beginning at the highest levels with the goals described in the President's National Security Strategy. At the departmental level, the Secretary of Defense articulates DoD's vision for achieving these security-related goals in the National Defense Strategy. This, in turn, leads to the generation of a variety of guidance documents, each focused on specific aspects of the strategy. These documents include the GEF and the derivative COCOM theater campaign plans, which, among other things, promulgate objectives tied directly to building capacity in partner countries for specific purposes.

Deriving Supporting Objectives and Purposes for BPC

As explained earlier in this chapter, purposes are specific military or interagency mission areas. High-level objectives and purposes or supporting objectives are linked by perceived threats or needs. In other words, the military planner observes a threat or need, and then determines a relevant objective. *Threats*, as the term is used in this report, are identifiable conditions within a country or region that create instability in the security sector. They demand resolution by military or similar means, and when a country cannot address the threat on its own, it may be appropriate for the United States or another entity to step in and help the country build its capacity to do so. For example, if a country with a poorly secured border perceives the threat of illicit trafficking, its planners may develop an objective related to securing the border. In the context of security cooperation, U.S. planners may develop an objective aimed at *assisting* the PN with securing its border. Needs might place a less immediate demand for resolution on the partner, yet addressing them can have a cross-cutting effect on how a partner military performs. Needs may include, for example, interoperability, defense institution building, and the ability to participate in coalition operations.

Supporting security cooperation objectives or purposes, such as border security or defense institution building, are derived from a variety of sources, including the *OSD Security Cooperation Toolkit* and the GEF. Because these are essentially broad military mission areas, they can be correlated with particular security cooperation programs. The supporting objectives or purposes associated with a particular security cooperation program can be obvious; program titles often reflect the main purpose the program is intended to support. For example, the Coalition Support Funds program is clearly intended to provide assistance to partner countries for participation in U.S.-led coalition operations.

Some programs are less obvious, simply because they can support so many objectives. The Chairman's Exercise Program can be used to work with partners for counterterrorism, disaster relief, counternarcotics, and many other purposes. Other programs are not obvious at all. The Antiterrorism Assistance Program, for example, is indeed used to provide antiterrorism assistance, but it may also be used for a variety of other purposes, such as border security, law enforcement, and countering weapons of mass destruction. Box 2.1 lists the security cooperation objectives of these types of programs.

Defense Sector Assessment Rating Tool

Developed as a way to identify gaps in a PN's defense needs, the DSART provides a methodical, repeatable way for planners to understand the threats that a country faces, potential approaches and means of assistance to fill those gaps, and the effectiveness of those efforts over time.[15] We used the DSART as the basis for an analytical method in our assessment of this study's historical BPC cases.

Box 2.1
Security Cooperation Objectives

Aviation expertise	Health
Border security	Humanitarian assistance
Coalition operations	Intelligence, surveillance, and reconnaissance
Countering weapons of mass destruction	Interoperability
Counterinsurgency	Law enforcement
Counternarcotics	Maritime security
Counterterrorism	Missile defense
Counter-threat financing	Peacekeeping
Cyber security	Port security
Defense institution building	Research and development
Demining	Stabilization and reconstruction
Disaster relief	

---

[15] See Agnes Gereben Schaefer, Lynn E. Davis, Ely Ratner, Molly Dunigan, Jeremiah Goulka, Heather Peterson, and K. Jack Riley, *Developing a Defense Sector Assessment Rating Tool*, Santa Monica, Calif.: RAND Corporation, TR-864-OSD, 2010.

The DSART was intended to provide DoD planners with a comprehensive understanding of the state of a country's defense sector. It considers a variety of factors and asks detailed questions, the answers to which reveal information about the basic characteristics of the country's defense sector, including its defense institutions and processes. Of particular interest for our study, however, were the detailed assessments of "critical functions." According to the tool, critical functions correspond to high-priority threats, including terrorism and insurgency, drug trafficking, porous land or sea borders, piracy, and instability in the aftermath of a conflict.[16]

Clearly, these functions relate directly to the security cooperation purposes and objectives discussed earlier. While the variety of purposes for which one might conduct BPC efforts is much wider, it is clear that these five do link to the high-priority threats included in the DSART.

Modifying the DSART

To account for the wide variety of potential security cooperation purposes and objectives in the individual case studies, we developed a modified version of the DSART's five critical functions to define the five BPC objective areas. These modified functions more comprehensively reflect the range of security cooperation objectives found in documents such as the GEF, and they also accommodate important efforts to build and strengthen relationships with PNs. Table 2.2 shows this modified set of functions.

The sixth category, "Relationship building or maintenance, securing access," is not related to any of the traditional DSART functions, nor is it clearly a capacity-related objective. However, it is an objective that is often pursued through the allocation of BPC activities and resources. In several instances in the case studies, improving relations or securing access was the primary objective of BPC activities; actually building PN defense capacity of any kind was a secondary or even tertiary goal.

Because of the ways in which relationship building differs from the other five (actual capacity building) objectives, we distinguish it

---

[16] Schaefer et al., 2010, p. 11.

Table 2.2
BPC Objectives: Modified DSART Functions

Category	Description
1	Internal security, including counterinsurgency, counterterrorism, and forces for counternarcotics
2	Conventional forces for self-defense and regional security, including air and missile defense and coalition operations
3	Specialty forces for external use, including counterterrorism, peacekeeping, peace enforcement, provision of humanitarian assistance, reconstruction, other stability operations, counterpiracy, and counternarcotics
4	Ministerial capacity, defense institution creation, and reform
5	Border security, along with maritime security, counterpiracy, countertrafficking, and crop eradication
A	Relationship building or maintenance, securing access

in the list with using a letter ("A") instead of a number to remind the reader that, while relationship building or access is a possible BPC objective, it is an orange among apples in relation to the other identified objectives.

Note that while we distinguish relationship building or access as a "non-capacity-building" objective, this distinction is not meant to be pejorative. We recognize that BPC is just one aspect of broader U.S. defense policy and U.S. foreign policy writ large and that relationship building or access is a potentially critical foreign policy goal, as suggested in the 2010 National Security Strategy. BPC is a perfectly reasonable way to pursue that goal.[17] We make the distinction only because of the narrow emphasis of this research on factors that are related to effectiveness in building capacity. By recognizing relationship building as an objective and treating it separately, we avoid misunderstanding and mislabeling a situation in which that was the central objective all along. Thus, if DoD spent a great deal on BPC and realized negligible improvements in objective categories 1–5 but achieved

[17] Office of the President of the United States, *National Security Strategy*, Washington, D.C., May 2010, p. 12.

outstanding success in category A, we were able to detect this objective in our case studies.

Each critical function or BPC objective area is represented by a number of subordinate factors, each scored from 1 to 5 as follows:

1. *very low:* entirely lacking
2. *low:* beginning to develop
3. *neither low nor high:* minimal but functioning
4. *high:* functional but room for improvement
5. *very high:* strong and no major improvement needed.

In our analysis, we used the average of all subordinate factors related to a critical function or BPC objective to produce the composite score for an objective area at a given point in time.

To identify appropriate subordinate factors for BPC assessment, we started with the subordinate factors for the DSART category closest to our modified DSART objective categories. We then made further modifications as needed to effectively capture the essence of that capability area. Box 2.2 lists the subordinate factors for modified DSART objective category 1, internal security. Importantly, many of these factors may only be addressed by DoD BPC efforts, such as training mili-

Box 2.2
Subordinate Factors for BPC Objective Category 1: Internal Security

Ability to train military forces for counterterrorism, counterinsurgency, or counternarcotics operations

Ability to carry out surveillance, reconnaissance, and intelligence operations

Ability to maintain security throughout the country, including protection of critical infrastructure; ability to prevent terrorist/insurgent attacks

Sufficient ministerial capacity to plan and integrate strategy and operations

Ability to combat corruption

Ability to police, prosecute, and incarcerate drug traffickers, terrorists, and insurgents

Ability to deploy rapid and mobile reaction capabilities

Logistics for, and maintenance and sustainment of, these capabilities

Ability to establish drug eradication and interdiction programs (conditional)

tary forces or deploying for rapid and mobile reaction. Others, obviously, can be addressed by other agencies.

When a factor is listed as "conditional," that indicates that its presence depends on the case. For example, the last subordinate factor in Box 2.2 concerns drug eradication; this factor's inclusion is conditional on the internal security issues that a BPC effort seeks to address as part of the counternarcotics mission. The appendix to this report lists the subordinate factors for all five capacity-related BPC objectives.

We can also see that the internal security BPC objective has nine supporting factors, one of which is conditional. If we assessed these factors in a country case on our 1–5 scale as 3, 3, 2, 2, 3, 3, 2, 2, and 1, then the modified DSART score for internal security at that point in time would be the average of those scores—in this case, 2.33.

Further details on how we used the modified DSART scores to assess the effectiveness of BPC historically, including a worked example from a specific (notional) case, can be found in Chapter Five.

Resourcing Activities to Build Partner Capacity

High-level threats, objectives, and purposes are simply the beginning of the BPC process. However, once the objective or objectives are identified, the security cooperation planner has to align resources, targeting the most appropriate security cooperation program from the many available.[18] In this section, we introduce security cooperation programs and activities and provide a set of examples to illustrate how they are used to build partner capabilities.

Deriving Requirements for Activities to Build Partner Capacity

Because security cooperation programs are typically designed with a specific purpose in mind, security cooperation planners can organize their efforts to build partner capacity by selecting appropriate pro-

---

[18] For a detailed discussion of specific security cooperation programs and their objectives, see Jennifer D. P. Moroney, Joe Hogler, Lianne Kennedy-Boudali, and Stephanie Pezard, *Integrating the Full Range of Security Cooperation Programs into Air Force Planning: An Analytic Primer*, Santa Monica, Calif.: RAND Corporation, TR-974-AF, 2011.

grams. Continuing with the earlier example, internal security, a security cooperation planner might try to draw on programs designed to assist the PN with border security. He or she might also consider programs with other, related objectives, such as counternarcotics, countering weapons of mass destruction, or even intelligence, surveillance, and reconnaissance.

Another consideration when developing a plan to build partner capacity is the method, or the way in which a program conducts its activities. Some programs are meant to transfer equipment, while others provide training. Some programs are collaborative in nature, while others are more of a one-way street. The way in which a program's activities are conducted has the greatest effect on how a partner's capability and capacity are developed. Activities such as conferences or workshops may be a good way to break the ice or expose a partner to new concepts, but training and equipping may lead to more concrete and immediate results.

In most cases, a combination of activities, sequenced in a logical way over time, is most effective in building capabilities and capacity. If a PN simply does not have the capability (or capabilities) to counter a threat, security cooperation efforts begin with building that capability. Where a capability exists in a PN's military, the planner may aim to improve and expand upon it, eventually building the partner's capacity.

BPC Activities: A Macro View

The U.S. government, primarily through DoS and DoD, pursues BPC activities in a number of ways. In some cases, equipment transfer might be the appropriate activity, along with training on how to operate or maintain it. In other cases, conducting combined exercises to develop or mature existing capabilities might be a desirable activity. Table 2.3 presents a set of activity types drawn largely from RAND work and DoD strategies. The activities are categorized as "nascent," "developing," or "advanced." These labels are intended as guidelines for selecting appropriate activities for specific partners.

If a particular partner has only a nascent relationship with the United States or with DoD, specifically, it may be best to select activities from the "nascent" list. These activities might also be appropriate

Table 2.3
BPC Activities Relative to Partner's Relationship with the United States

Nascent	Developing	Advanced
Needs/capabilities assessments	Education	Personnel exchanges
Training	Exercises	Research, development, test, and evaluation
Conferences, workshops	Equipment	Experimentation
Information exchanges	Construction	Provide air-/sealift
Defense/military contacts	Supplies	

for countries with a lesser ability to absorb assistance, or those with a relatively technically unsophisticated military. The idea is that more capable, stable partners with more robust U.S. relationships will be more suitable candidates for "developing" or even "advanced" activities. Of course, objectives and purposes may dictate otherwise. Moreover, these activities should not be thought of in a linear way or as sequential in nature. For example, needs assessments are routinely conducted as part of any program, both as an initial step and as a recurring activity to assess progress toward objectives. As Figure 2.1 illustrates, the activities are nested so that developing activities subsume nascent activities, and both nascent and developing activities are subsumed by advanced activities.

BPC Activities: An Illustration

In this section, we describe BPC activities in specific country contexts, illustrating the ways in which the United States goes about building partner capacity. The examples, while simplified, introduce the BPC processes used by the United States; they are described in context in the case studies presented later in this report.

The following examples are drawn from five regional COCOMs: USEUCOM (U.S. European Command), USPACOM (U.S. Pacific Command), USCENTCOM, USSOUTHCOM, and USAFRICOM (U.S. Africa Command). As shown in Table 2.4, we start with the

Figure 2.1
Relationships Among BPC Activities

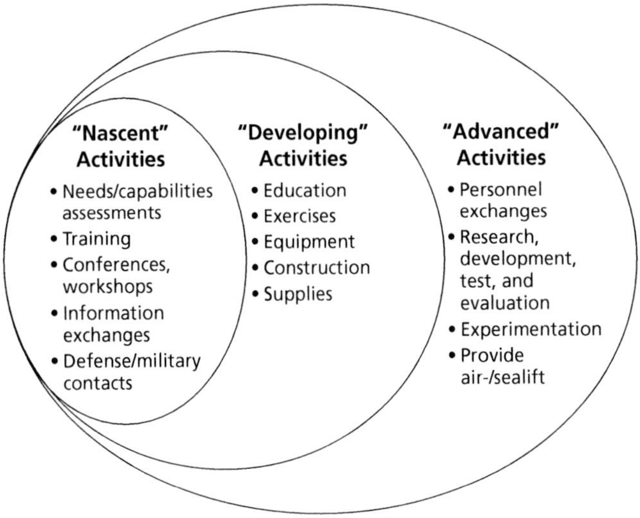

RAND *MG1253/1-2.1*

specific BPC activity, link the activity to a specific country, present the relevant modified DSART functions, and describe the authorities and assistance provided.

Train and Equip: Building Partner Capacity to Address a Threat

The first two examples in Table 2.4 focus on efforts undertaken by the United States to build partner capacity to meet specific threats through the provision of training and equipment. In the first example, the United States worked to address Colombia's capacity to conduct counterterrorism and counterinsurgency operations. The equipment and training provided to Colombia links to the following modified DSART categories: (1) internal security and (5) border security. "Plan Colombia" was initially designed to assist that country in addressing the problem of narcotrafficking. Over time, the United States began to provide assistance to address the dual threats of insurgency and narcotrafficking. Under the USSOUTHCOM area of responsibility, Plan Colombia began in 2000 to train and equip Colombian commando battalions for counterinsurgency and counternarcotics operations in

Table 2.4
Summary of Examples

Activity	COCOM	Country	Threat or Need	Modified DSART Functions/BPC Objectives	Authorities, Funding
Training, equipment	USSOUTHCOM	Colombia	Narcotrafficking Insurgency	1. Internal security 5. Border security	Title 10 and Title 22 authorities; various funding sources, but primarily counternarcotics and security assistance
Training, equipment	USPACOM	Philippines	Insurgency Terrorism	1. Internal security 5. Border security A. Relationship building	Title 10 and Title 22 authorities; counterterrorism funding and security assistance
Training, equipment	USEUCOM	Georgia	Interoperability	3. Specialty forces 4. Ministerial capacity	Title 10 and 22 authorities; various funding sources over multiple phases
Training	USAFRICOM	Senegal	Peacekeeping	3. Specialty forces	Title 22, global peacekeeping operations initiative
Exercise	USCENTCOM	Kyrgyzstan	Interoperability Border security	4. Ministerial capacity 5. Border security A. Relationship building	Title 10 authorities; USCENTCOM Regional Cooperation exercise focused on disaster management

the domestic arena. This effort involved the U.S. Army and other services; contractors conducted needs assessments and provided technical training and direct support for materiel. From 2000 to 2005, when the program officially ended, the country received more than $6 billion in U.S. aid through Plan Colombia, a level of commitment that has been exceeded only by U.S. training and assistance efforts in Iraq and Afghanistan. Training efforts focused on human rights training, as well as airpower, intelligence, communication, and interdiction capabilities. The main sources of funding for security assistance were IMET and FMF, along with the Andean Counterdrug Initiative.[19]

Training and equipment activities were also conducted with the Philippines to address terrorist and insurgent threats there. Conducted in the USPACOM area of responsibility, Operation Enduring Freedom–Philippines (OEF-P) began in May 2003 and is ongoing as of this writing. The aim of the program is to train and equip Philippine forces to counter the activities of terrorist groups—particularly the Islamist separatist Abu Sayyaf Group—on a domestic scale and to deny safe haven to al Qaida operatives in the region. These objectives link to the following modified DSART functions: (1) internal security, (5) border security, and (A) relationship building.

The U.S.-led OEF-P is executed by Special Operations Command Pacific; contractors are not involved. At the height of OEF-P, fiscal years (FYs) 2001–2004, security cooperation resources totaled $180 million from FMF, IMET, and DoD drawdown. In FY 2005, the FMF share was just under $30 million, and IMET funds totaled $3 million.[20] OEF-P units were trained in light infantry, night flying operations, combat and humanitarian engineering, and intelligence capabilities, and the United States provided equipment to support those training initiatives. Maritime equipment for interdiction purposes, radars for adjacent border surveillance, UH-1 Huey helicopters,

---

[19] IMET and FMF funding levels were more than $100 million for fiscal year 2006, while Andean Counterdrug Initiative funding was $463,000. See U.S. Department of State, Bureau of Political-Military Affairs, *Colombia: Security Assistance*, Washington, D.C., October 17, 2008.

[20] The level of IMET funds allocated to the Philippines is the largest in Asia and second largest in the world.

and precision-guided missiles are a few examples of the equipment provided to the Philippines using 1206 funds.[21] Overall, the effort has been useful in assisting the government of the Philippines in addressing terrorist and insurgent threats. Relationship-building efforts have been less productive, however, largely because of the Philippine government's resistance to allowing access and engaging in relationship-building activities. Such activities often have political dimensions that either help or hinder the achievement of objectives.

Train and Equip: Building Partner Capacity to Address a Need

The third example in Table 2.4 illustrates how the same type of activities, training, and provision of equipment can be used to achieve a different objective. After initially working with the Georgians to address insurgency threats in the Pankisi Gorge, the focus of DoD assistance shifted to interoperability with U.S.-led coalition forces. Specifically, the United States conducted BPC activities with Georgia to enhance interoperability for deployments to Iraq and Afghanistan. In the USEUCOM area of responsibility, Georgia is a fairly unique case in that resources were combined to form three large-scale BPC efforts. The Georgia Train and Equip Program ran from May 2002 to April 2004. It was followed by a second BPC effort, the Sustainment and Stability Operations Program, from April 2005 to June 2006, and a third, the Georgia Deployment Program, which was ongoing as of this writing. These efforts link to the following modified DSART functions: (3) specialty forces for external use and (4) ministerial capacity.

The latter two efforts, the Sustainment and Stability Operations Program and the Georgia Deployment Program, were designed specifically to train Georgian forces to assist in Operation Iraqi Freedom.[22] Marine Forces Europe led the training with contractor support. Two infantry battalions, two logistics battalions, and signal, reconnaissance, and engineer brigade companies were trained and equipped, as were

---

[21] Nina M. Serafino, *Security Assistance Reform: "Section 1206," Background and Issues for Congress*, Washington, D.C.: Congressional Research Service, RS22855, January 13, 2012, p. 24.

[22] The focus was on Georgia's 1st Infantry Brigade.

the Georgian Land Forces Command Staff and an operations cell from the General Staff. Like the Georgia Train and Equip Program, these programs drew on many different funding sources, including FMF, IMET, Peacekeeping Operations funds, and Coalition Support Funds, totaling about $130 million. In FY 2010–2011, $42 million in 1206 funding was allocated to Georgia.

Training: Why Building Partner Capacity Is Not Always Effective

In the fourth example in Table 2.4, we again consider how training can help build a partner military's capacity—or, to be more precise, how it can fail to do so. In this case, the United States, working with other partners and allies, provided peacekeeping training to Senegal.[23] This effort links to modified DSART function (3) specialty forces for external use. Although Senegal is in the USAFRICOM area of responsibility, much of the primary peacekeeping and peace support operations training was conducted at the Italian Center of Excellence for Stability Police Units (CoESPU) in Vicenza. The Italian government established CoESPU in March 2005 with funding support from the United States and other G-8 countries. Its mission is to train foreign military and civilian police units in law enforcement techniques, with expertise provided by Italy's Arma dei Carabinieri gendarme force.[24]

CoESPU offers two courses, one for high-level personnel and another for middle management, with both classroom and field components. CoESPU trainees receive training in international organizations, international law, military arts in peace support operations, tactical doctrine, operating in mixed international environments with hybrid chains of command, and the selection, training, and organization of police units for international peace support operations. The primary focus of these courses is on "training the trainers," who will return to their home country and train other officers there. It is not

---

23 As well as to many other African partner militaries.

24 CoESPU is part of the G-8's Global Peace Operations Initiative. For more information, see Nina N. Serafino, *The Global Peace Operations Initiative: Background and Issues for Congress*, Washington, D.C.: Congressional Research Service, RL32773, June 11, 2009.

clear that this is actually happening, however. In many cases, the recipient countries fail to build on the initial training received at CoESPU.

Despite the less-than-hoped-for results, DoD supports CoESPU through the Global Peace Operations Initiative and provides a U.S. colonel to fill the position of CoESPU's deputy director.[25] However, because DoS controls the resources, DoD has not been heavily engaged in CoESPU policy and programmatic matters. Instead, the DoS Bureau of Political-Military Affairs is the U.S. program manager for the Global Peace Operations Initiative and the primary interlocutor with the Italian Ministry of Foreign Affairs and Ministry of Defense on CoESPU matters, such as selecting countries to receive training.

Exercises: Demonstrating a Partner's Capacity to Address a Threat

In the final example in Table 2.4, we consider exercise-related BPC in Kyrgyzstan in the USCENTCOM area of responsibility. For about a decade, USCENTCOM has held an annual exercise (typically with a tabletop and a field component) in Central Asia called Regional Cooperation, and Kyrgyzstan is a key participant. The exercise enables regional information sharing in counterterrorism, humanitarian assistance, and disaster response. The focus is on regional issues that crosscut borders. The objectives of Regional Cooperation link to the following modified DSART functions: (4) ministerial capacity, (5) border security, and (A) relationship building. While the scenarios vary from year to year, the exercise usually includes a natural or man-made disaster. The primary output of the exercise is the increased capacity to operate regionally with partner countries—an important objective in a region with historically poor ties among its countries. Regional Cooperation has helped identify capability and information-sharing deficiencies in the host nation as well as within the other participating countries (e.g., Kazakhstan, Uzbekistan, Pakistan). Resolving those shortfalls, in turn, may facilitate other capacity-building activities with the participating PNs.

---

[25] The deputy director position was filled by a U.S. Army O-6 from 2007 to 2009 and by a U.S. Marine Corps O-6 from 2009 to 2011.

Summary

The BPC process is complex and will vary from country to country and from situation to situation. Threats drive security-focused objectives, and related programs are tapped to conduct activities that build the capabilities and capacities with partner countries. The results of such efforts can be assessed. Using analytical tools, such as the DSART, we considered actual historical cases of BPC, assessing the effectiveness of these initiatives and attempting to identify lessons for future efforts. The following chapter presents the hypotheses that guided our analysis.

CHAPTER THREE

Hypotheses and Factors: What Works Best for Building Partner Capacity, and Under What Circumstances?

Chapter Two provided an overview of U.S. BPC efforts, describing the types of activities conducted under the BPC rubric and the categories of objectives that can be pursued with BPC. This chapter begins to explore factors that might influence, or that at least correlate with, different degrees of effectiveness in capacity building.

Obviously, some programs and activities are more effective for capacity building: Some properties of programs or activities increase or decrease effectiveness, some conditions or contextual factors make certain BPC easier or harder, and certain combinations of activities, activity features, and contextual factors interact to make BPC more or less effective. Personnel who work or have worked in BPC planning or execution have an intuitive sense of what works and what does not—and what conditions are more or less favorable for BPC. This project seeks to test and validate these intuitive beliefs with a broad empirical foundation. This chapter presents our formal hypotheses, many derived from common sense or from the experiences of those involved in planning or executing BPC, which we tested through this research effort.

Identifying Hypotheses and Factors

What makes BPC more effective or less effective? Notions of constraints and correlates abound among practitioners and in documented discussions. To gather a preliminary set of hypotheses about inputs or conditions (contextual factors) that might have contributed to or diminished the effectiveness of BPC historically, we cast a wide net. We gathered preliminary hypotheses from the following sources:

- existing RAND research in the broader area of security cooperation and the expertise and experience of the project team[1]
- discussions with sponsor points of contact and stakeholders who attended interim project briefings
- inductive observations from the individual cases. (If the early narrative for a case suggested that a certain factor or factors were critical in that case, we hypothesized that those factors could be critical in other cases, and thus developed a generalizable hypothesis based on the single observed instance.)

We then refined our lengthy preliminary list of candidate hypotheses in several ways. First, we combined, organized, and categorized hypotheses, reducing the overall number by eliminating redundancy and then grouping them under thematic "parent" hypotheses, often as a host of corollary hypotheses. Second, we considered whether or not candidate hypotheses were likely to be testable with the types and levels of data we expected to collect as part of the case studies, eliminating those for which we did not expect to be able to collect sufficient evidence. In doing so, we perhaps erred on the side of inclusivity; ultimately, several of the hypotheses that we carried forward into the research could not be tested with the data collected, usually because

[1] Several members of the project team have considerable research experience in security cooperation. See, for example, Jennifer D. P. Moroney, Beth Grill, Joe Hogler, Lianne Kennedy-Boudali, and Christopher Paul, *How Successful Are U.S. Efforts to Build Capacity in Developing Countries? A Framework to Assess the Global Train and Equip "1206" Program*, Santa Monica, Calif.: RAND Corporation, TR-1121-OSD, 2011; Jennifer D. P. Moroney, Joe Hogler, Jefferson P. Marquis, Christopher Paul, John E. Peters, Beth Grill, *Developing an Assessment Framework for U.S. Air Force Building Partnerships Programs*, Santa Monica, Calif.: RAND Corporation, MG-868-AF, 2010; Moroney, Hogler, et al., 2011; Jennifer D. P. Moroney, Adam Grissom, and Jefferson P. Marquis, *A Capabilities-Based Strategy for Army Security Cooperation*, Santa Monica, Calif.: RAND Corporation, MG-563-A, 2007; and Jennifer D. P. Moroney and Joe Hogler, with Benjamin Bahney, Kim Cragin, David R. Howell, Charlotte Lynch, and S. Rebecca Zimmerman, *Building Partner Capacity to Combat Weapons of Mass Destruction*, Santa Monica, Calif.: RAND Corporation, MG-783-DTRA, 2009.

we were unable to consistently obtain data of sufficient detail across all cases (see Box 3.1). This was the final way in which hypotheses were downselected.

For the refined list of project hypotheses and corollaries, we next sought to represent each with factors or variables that we could collect for each phase of each case (the phasing for cases is described in Chapter Four). Because of the analytic requirements of qualitative comparative analysis (QCA, described in Chapter Five), our preference and first cut for desired variables consisted of binary factors—factors that could be scored as present (1) or absent (0) for each phase of each case. An

Box 3.1
Discarded Hypotheses

The following is a list of hypotheses that we carried forward into the analysis but could not reach conclusions on, either because the data collected ultimately failed to represent the constructs implied in the hypotheses or because we could not collect data with which to test these hypotheses with sufficient consistency. We present them here for reference and because they might have utility for further research.

- The more "skin in the game" a PN has (in terms of money, personnel, other resources), the more committed it is and the more effective BPC is.
- BPC efforts are less effective with conscript forces.
- BPC efforts are less durable/sustainable with conscript forces.
- PNs emerging from conflict or that are highly dependent on the United States are more cooperative.
- Lack of consistency/predictability can reduce PN motivation and sour the relationship if "promises aren't kept."
- BPC efforts that are part of a broad-based and integrated "whole-of-government" approach in a PN (USAID, DoS, DoD) are more effective.
- Exercises/collaboration with immediate neighbors or regional coalitions positively affects PN capacity.
- Military-to-military contact is more effective in building relationships than contractor-to-military contact.
- Specialty forces or forces specifically designed for BPC are more effective than general-purpose forces in delivering BPC.
- BPC efforts are more effective when the partner forces are similar to the provider forces (i.e., military-to-military vs. military-to-police).
- Focused mobile training teams for individual units are more effective than large-scale exercises.
- "Prestige buys" or ceremonial or parade force development have little impact on actual capacity built.

example would be "PN facing significant security challenge," which would be scored 1 (present) if the partner was indeed facing a significant security challenge in that phase or 0 (absent) if it was not.

The second class of factors we sought were either continuous or categorical. These included all factors that could not be represented as binary data and that followed the traditional denotation for different types of variables. Continuous variables include factors with meaningful numerical scales, such as "Total dollars (in millions) spent on BPC in phase" or "Average World Bank Governance Indicator percentile rank in phase." Categorical variables were factors that assigned a case phase to either an ordinal category (high, medium, low) or an explanatory category (lack of logistic support, insufficient training, inadequate equipment). Examples include "Primary DSART objective categories for phase" and "Reason partner absorptive capacity is low."

The final class of factors we sought consisted of constructed variables. We did not collect these directly; rather, we built them by combining or evaluating other factors. For example, "Defense spending as a fraction of gross domestic product (GDP)" would take the continuous factors "Average PN spending on defense" and "Average PN GDP" for a phase and combine them. Some of these constructed variables were more or less complex. We sought to identify a preliminary set of constructed variables to represent various hypotheses when developing those hypotheses and the desired data list. In practice, during the analytical phase, we constructed considerably more factors than we had initially planned (though certainly no more than is typical in quantitative data analysis).

Study Hypotheses and Factors

This section presents the study hypotheses and corollary hypotheses, as well as the factors chosen to represent the hypotheses in the case-study data. The hypotheses are listed under four numbered parent hypotheses, each of which is assumed to have some face validity and was not explicitly tested. The corollary hypotheses, each listed with a number (which corresponds to its parent hypothesis) and letter (to distinguish it from other corollaries), were explicitly tested in the analyses presented in Chapter Five. The four parent hypotheses are as follows:

1. The way in which the United States plans, resources, and executes BPC influences effectiveness.
2. You can lead a horse to water but you cannot make it drink: Low partner motivation is adverse to capacity outcomes.
3. PN baseline capabilities (in government, economy, and defense) influence the effectiveness of BPC.
4. The broader context (the geopolitical situation, other neighbors and partners) influences the effectiveness of BPC.

All four of the parent hypotheses were validated in the analysis (which is unsurprising). The detailed results of the corollary hypotheses, however, are of the greatest interest. In the following sections, we enumerate each corollary hypothesis.

Parent hypothesis 1: The way in which the United States plans, resources, and executes BPC influences effectiveness.

H1a: The more money you spend, the more partner capacity you build.

This hypothesis is one part minimal hypothesis (Do expenditures correlate with activities, and do activities correlate with capacity building?) and one part genuine inquiry (Just how strongly do expenditures correlate with effectiveness?). **Factors:** Total dollars (in millions) spent on BPC in phase;[2] various constructed variables, including average

2 We calculated expenditures in two different ways. First, we examined all BPC funding that we were able to identify, along with the FMS and DCS net of FMF, to get an accurate assessment of the total amount spent on U.S. BPC. The inclusion of FMS and DCS reflects the PN's financial contribution to U.S. BPC. We deducted the FMF amount from FMS because FMS often comes with a matched FMF case. (Specifically, the United States sells a PN certain materiel or support but then also provides a grant to pay for it.) This step was necessary to avoid double counting (because FMF funds were part of our BPC expenditure baseline). Second, we used these lower-level expenditures to capture just the U.S. contribution, excluding FMS and DCS.

BPC expenditures per year and various transformations of expenditures (such as the log transformation).[3]

H1b: Where relationship building/access is a primary objective, capacity outcomes may not correlate well with expenditures/ efforts.

This hypothesis explicitly tests the impact of a complexity of BPC that we noted earlier in this report. Specifically, in many cases, BPC activities are not conducted solely to build capacity; they sometimes contribute to other foreign policy goals, like improving relationships or seeking or maintaining access to PNs for overflight, transshipment, or basing. When these non–capacity-related objectives are among the primary objectives, this hypothesis suggests that actual capacity building may suffer, even if overall foreign policy objectives are well served. **Factor:** Relationship building/access as a primary BPC objective.

H1c: . . . and that is OK.

This is not really a hypothesis—more of an assumption or observation. Evidence supporting H1b does not suggest anything negative about BPC; H1c is simply an acknowledgment that sometimes BPC programs and activities are used in pursuit of goals (such as access or relationship building) that have nothing directly to do with partner defense capacity. Successful use of BPC to pursue important non–capacity-related goals is a positive outcome, and we want to be careful not to judge such instances harshly for less effective capacity building if capacity building was not really the goal. There are no explicit factors for this hypothesis.

---

[3] One transforms data in statistical analysis to make a curved relationship (such as an asymptotic relationship, or a curve showing diminishing returns) into a linear relationship (which many statistical procedures, including regression, assume). The log (or logarithm) transformation referred to in this case simply takes the log of the dollar value of BPC in $ millions. So, if a country received $58.3 million in a phase, we would instead use log (58.3) = 1.766 as the expenditure value. Doing this for all country phases creates a much more linear relationship between effectiveness and expenditures.

H1d: Consistency produces better results; stable, designated resources improve the likelihood of reaching objectives.

Other studies have reported significant inconsistency in the funding and delivery of BPC to some countries and indicated that this slows and impedes capacity development. This hypothesis proposes that a clear and consistent stream of funding and activities, rather than activities that start and stop or funding that comes in fits and spurts, is more effective. **Factors:** BPC funding relatively consistent from year to year; average delta in funding from year to year (in $ millions); primary BPC activity relatively consistent from year to year; BPC activities suspended temporarily or otherwise delivered disjointedly in this phase.

H1e: Incorporating sustainment considerations into the effort increases the likelihood of the partner retaining the capability.

This hypothesis builds from concerns raised about BPC activities that create capability but include no effort to sustain that capability, be it in the form of an arrangement for maintenance or logistics support for provided equipment, refresher training, or continued financial support. H1e surmises that BPC efforts that include some kind of sustainment effort will be more likely to be retained by the partner and thus more effective over time. **Factor:** Most significant BPC efforts include a significant sustainment/retention component.

H1f: Temporary punitive funding decrements have modest adverse consequences for BPC efforts.

With some regularity, Congress will suspend certain forms of aid to countries, including funding for some BPC activities, because of human rights violations or other breaches of international behavioral norms. This hypothesis asserts that such interruptions, even if relatively short, impede BPC efforts. **Factors:** Phase included a temporary punitive funding decrement; BPC activities suspended temporarily or otherwise delivered disjointedly in the phase.

H1g: Long-term punitive funding decrements have lasting adverse consequences for partner capacity.

H1g follows from H1f and suggests that lengthy punitive interruptions will impede BPC, even if short interruptions do not. **Factor:** Phase included (or is defined by) a lengthy punitive reduction in BPC funding and support.

H1h: Punitive funding decrements can provide leverage and improve behaviors that resulted in the funding cut.

H1h addresses a slightly different question—specifically, whether punitive funding decrements adversely affect BPC or whether they lead to improved behavior by partners. The hypothesis proposes that they do. **Factors:** Phase included a temporary punitive funding decrement; phase included (or is defined by) a lengthy punitive reduction in BPC funding and support; evidence that punitive funding cut led to improved behavior by PN.

Parent hypothesis 2: You can lead a horse to water but you cannot make it drink: Low partner motivation is adverse to capacity outcomes.

H2a: Differences between PN and U.S. BPC goals reduce effectiveness.

This hypothesis simply proposes that if the United States and the PN want different outcomes from BPC efforts, effectiveness is likely to be reduced. An example would be if the United States wanted to help build specialty forces for peacekeeping duties (DSART objective 3: specialty forces for external use) but the PN really wanted to build internal security forces (DSART objective 1) or simply did not particularly want to build peacekeeping forces. **Factors:** PN BPC goals/desires differ substantially from U.S. goals; capability built clearly aligns with PN objectives.

H2b: BPC efforts are more successful when U.S. and PN strategic aims align/when BPC efforts address areas of mutual concern.

H2b makes the fairly obvious connection between shared interests and prospects for success, considering the alignment of broader strategic interests or BPC focused in areas of mutual concern, or both. **Factors:** Primary BPC effort supports area of concern to both the PN and the United States; U.S. and PN interests in the region predominantly align. **Constructed factor:** Strategic interests align *and* the BPC effort targets an area of mutual concern.

H2c: Capacity built to meet PN objectives is more likely to be sustained/used by the partner.

Independent of shared interests and U.S. interests, H2c suggests greater effectiveness if the PN wants it and if the effort meets the PN's objectives. **Factors:** Capability built clearly aligns with PN objectives; PN BPC goals/desires differ substantially from U.S. goals; evidence that capabilities built through BPC were being used for purposes other than intended.

H2d: Partners that invest their own funds to maintain capability, conduct training, or invest in maintenance programs will have more success.

This hypothesis returns explicitly to motivation, suggesting a lack of demonstration of commitment through an investment in sustaining the BPC effort. This reflects a lack of motivation, which, in turn, influences effectiveness. **Factor:** Substantial investment by PN in developing or maintaining capabilities.

H2e: BPC efforts with a PN with a demonstrated commitment to national defense are more effective.

H2e considers only the demonstration of motivation for defense without explicitly connecting motivation to BPC. **Factors:** Average annual defense spending by partner (in $ millions); PN's average annual GDP (in $ millions). **Constructed factor:** PN's average defense spending as a percentage of GDP.

H2f: Effective capacity building leads to effective relationship building.

While H1b notes that relationships can be built *instead of* capacity, H2f takes a different tack and suggests that good relationships correlate with effective capacity. Note that these are not mutually exclusive hypotheses. H1b indicates that capacity building may suffer when relationships are the primary goal, and H2f implies that capacity building may suffer if relationships are not sufficiently attended to. **Factors:** Relationship with PN is poor/low, adequate, or good; relationship with PN improved, improved dramatically, deteriorated, or remained stable.

Parent hypothesis 3: PN baseline capabilities (in government, economy, and defense) influence the effectiveness of BPC.

H3a: Willing but otherwise unprepared partners have lower absorptive capacity, limiting the effectiveness of BPC.

This hypothesis suggests that even if a partner is well motivated, it may be limited by its ability to absorb BPC. One can imagine many possible reasons for low absorptive capacity, including insufficient baseline training, low literacy or education, a lack of logistical support, inadequate equipment, a lack of defense institutions, or low levels of military professionalism. **Factors:** PN absorptive capacity is low; the reason that PN absorptive capacity is low.

H3b: Activities matched to partner baseline capabilities and absorptive capacity increase the effectiveness of BPC efforts.

Related to and adding nuance to H3a, this hypothesis considers the extent to which BPC activities match the baseline capabilities of PN forces, whether their absorptive capacity is low or not. **Factor:** Mismatch between PN absorptive capacity/baseline capability and BPC activities conducted.

H3c: BPC efforts are more effective with democratic partners who have relatively positive governance indicators.

This hypothesis starts with the premise that the quality and character of a PN's government and governance matter for BPC, proposing specifically that the degree of democratization and the strength of governance indicators affect BPC (for example, on international indexes of "voice," accountability, political stability and the absence of violence, government effectiveness, regulatory quality, rule of law, and control of corruption). **Factors:** Average World Bank Governance Indicator percentile rank in phase; PN is a mature democracy; PN is a partial or transitional democracy; PN government is competent; World Bank Corruption Index improved over the phase; World Bank Corruption

Index worsened over the phase; average World Bank Corruption Index for phase; PN includes significant ungoverned or lightly governed areas.

H3d: Disputed leadership leads to worse outcomes.

Several early case narratives reported profound disruptions in capacity building when PNs entered government crises or leadership disputes. H3d seeks to test this observation across all such instances. **Factor:** PN has disputed leadership/government crisis at any point in phase.

H3e: BPC will be more effective with partners that have reasonably strong/healthy economies.

While several previous hypotheses have looked to partner investment in BPC as evidence of PN motivation, H3e looks simply at the overall strength of the partner's economy, connecting the ability of the partner to fund and support BPC to effectiveness. **Factor:** Health of PN economy (United Nations Human Development Index average over period).

Parent hypothesis 4: The broader context (the geopolitical situation, other neighbors and partners) influences the effectiveness of BPC.

H4a:* Allegro non troppo: *The United States wants some partners to gain capacity—but not too much capacity—for a regional balance of power; when this is the case, outcomes may be capped relative to inputs.

Allegro non troppo is Italian for "happy but not too happy" and is the perfect turn of phrase to capture situations in which the United States seeks to build a partner's defense capacity—within certain limits. These limits may be imposed for reasons related to the regional balance of power, perhaps because a neighbor of the partner is also an ally that the United States does not want to threaten, or because of limits on U.S. trust in the reliability of the partner or the partner's forces (for example, if the United States is arming a partner's internal security forces to combat transnational terrorists but fears that these forces have been penetrated by a terrorist organization and that technologies or capabilities might be transferred to an adversary). In such a situation, BPC efforts should still build capacity, but, by design, effectiveness may lag what is expected simply by observing the inputs.[4] **Factor:** Practical limit on the amount of capacity that the United States desires to build.

H4b: BPC efforts of other countries can work at "cross-purposes" with U.S. BPC efforts, either by monopolizing elite troops and resources or by distracting the PN from the desired U.S. focus.

Inasmuch as U.S. BPC efforts cannot claim all the credit for capacity built in a country if other partners are also undertaking BPC activities, this hypothesis acknowledges that the BPC efforts of other countries—especially non-ally countries—might constrain the effectiveness of U.S. BPC. **Factors:** Other major country providing PN with more average BPC funding than United States in phase; other major country providing BPC support to PN is not a U.S. ally; other country's BPC efforts detracted from U.S. BPC efforts (distracted PN from U.S. objectives, monopolized PN elite troops or resources).

H4c: 9/11 was a watershed that made U.S. BPC more focused; post-9/11 BPC is more effective.

Early accounts of BPC from the post–Cold War but pre-9/11 era suggested that such efforts lacked focus. Post-9/11 BPC was certainly better-funded. This hypothesis suggests a sea change in the effectiveness of BPC after 9/11. **Factor:** Post-9/11 phase.

---

[4] As phrased, this factor is somewhat tautological: When the United States seeks to build less capacity, it builds less capacity. We include this hypothesis not so much to test it as to point it out and control for it. If we did not include a factor about limits to the desired level of capacity in our model, we might misidentify a situation in which the United States exactly met its BPC objectives as a situation in which BPC was ineffective.

CHAPTER FOUR

Historical Cases and Case Selection

This report presents our findings regarding BPC activities, their effectiveness, and the contexts in which they were undertaken in 29 case-study countries. Each case spans the 20-year period from 1990 to 2009—so, beginning with the end of the Cold War. This chapter describes how the cases were selected and provides information about the data collection efforts that informed our analysis. To protect the sensitivity of some details of the partnerships, this report does not list the 29 selected partners. However, we do rely on examples drawn from the less sensitive of the cases, as well as examples of other partnerships with which the authors are familiar. The full case studies can be found in the controlled-access companion report of the same title, which is available to those with a need to know and appropriate clearances.

Case Selection

The United States conducts some kind of BPC effort with the vast majority of countries in the world. Our preliminary explorations revealed that at least 184 countries were involved in BPC activities between 1999 and 2009. Lacking sufficient resources to conduct 184 (or more) case studies, we faced a challenge in narrowing this total to an appropriate subset of cases.

There is, of course, the traditional solution to a methodological situation in which the whole population can be identified but only a fraction of that population can be studied: some form of random sampling. We elected not to sample randomly for several reasons. First and foremost, while most of the world's countries participate in or receive some kind of BPC support from the United States, they are not all equally important. Random sampling would be as likely as not to give us cases that were mostly insignificant (recipients of minimal amounts of BPC) while—randomly and unintentionally, to be sure—excluding partners of critical importance. Second, we recognized at the outset of the project that assessing BPC outcomes—that is, whether or not and to what extent capacity was built—was going to be tricky. Cases selected randomly might be cases in which capacity built was obvious or easy to measure or assess, but such cases might also be opaque or minimally documented, or capacity built might have been so modest as to be difficult to discern at all.

The solution to this challenge was simple: Finding out more about *all* the possible cases allowed us to exclude those with analytically problematic properties (e.g., recipients of negligible or minimal BPC, partners for which capacity would be difficult to measure, cases with other identifiable but problematic characteristics) and those that were otherwise unattractive. This solution contained the seeds of another challenge, however: Identifying salient characteristics of candidate cases takes research time, and we had limited time in which to choose cases and begin our research. We certainly could have spent a significant proportion of our time and resources learning about BPC in 184 countries to weed out cases that were the least likely to be informative, but we would have risked not being able to complete a sufficient number of actual case studies in sufficient detail. Instead, we did a "quick-and-dirty" winnowing of the candidate cases.

We used three criteria to winnow the cases. This chapter has already alluded to the first criterion: We wanted more important or higher-priority cases in our final subset, and we believed that expenditures were a good indicator of importance. We had already identified BPC-related funding data for all countries from 1999 to 2009,[1] so we

---

[1] The data were from a series of reports to Congress by DoS and DoD (U.S. Department of State and U.S. Department of Defense, *Foreign Military Training and DoD Engagement Activities of Interest*, fiscal years 1999–2009, Washington, D.C., 2000–2009). We used the DoD-only subset, which excludes all programs administered by DoS (FMS, FMF, and IMET), the U.S. Department of Homeland Security, and the U.S. Coast Guard. The

chose to use those data to identify priority cut-offs. Second, we wanted to maximize our chances of being able to observe and measure or assess capacity. Our case selection process preceded the modification of the DSART for use in scoring BPC outcomes (see Chapter Two), so we still needed a way to measure capacity. At that point in the research process, the only sure way we knew a country could demonstrate defense capacity was through a deployment. Deployments are reasonably well documented, and even deploying in a permissive environment with noncombat duties exposes forces to external scrutiny that they do not receive at home in garrison. Finally, in consultation with our sponsor, we decided as our third criterion to exclude high-end partners. The core questions of this study are about effectiveness in building capacity, presumably where capacity was lacking. The emphasis here is not on countries that already have very high capacity, nor is it on building capacity for interoperability.

With these three criteria in mind, we sought data to identify thresholds that would either eliminate unattractive cases from the population so that we could sample randomly with higher confidence of getting only "good" cases or just sufficiently reduce the size of the case population. This latter outcome is what we were able to achieve.

First, we eliminated all "high-end" partners.[2] We used a combination of Eurozone members and a sensitive draft DoD list of "key equivalent" partners to exclude 21 high-end U.S. partners.

Second, we identified two spending priority thresholds: Top-priority countries, those on which the United States had spent at least $25 million in BPC between 1999 and 2009, according to our data,

preliminary funding data that we used to select the cases do not necessarily match the funding levels indicated elsewhere in the report, as the latter are more comprehensive.

2 High-end partners all have considerable baseline defense capabilities and considerable resources with which to build their own capabilities. Security cooperation with high-end partners is more about interoperability and jointly exercising multinational capabilities. While improving and exercising interoperability is important, the focus here is on building capacity from lower baselines.

and significant partners, those that received at least $5 million in U.S. BPC between 1999 and 2009.[3]

Third, we used international deployment data to identify the number of times each country deployed military forces outside its own borders since 1990 and at what strength, ultimately considering countries that made multiple deployments of at least company strength (~100+ troops).

Ultimately, we combined these three criteria as follows: We added countries that were high-priority funding recipients but were not top-tier partners (19 countries). Then, we included the countries that had multiple external deployments (two or more) of at least company strength, but were not top-tier partners (43 countries). Finally, we removed countries that had multiple deployments but were not significant partners, receiving less than $5 million in U.S. BPC between 1999 and 2009 (–22 countries). Nine countries were both high-priority recipients and deployed at least twice, so they qualified two ways. Thus, our case selection stood at 19 + 43 – 22 – 9 (for redundancy) = 31. The 31 selected countries included both Iraq and Afghanistan. U.S. operations in Iraq and Afghanistan have gone far beyond typical efforts to build partner defense capacity and include or included actual U.S. military operations; support for disarmament, demobilization, and reintegration; economic and governmental reconstruction; and more. Because disentangling "just" BPC activities from the host of other combat, combat support, security, and development activities in those countries would be incredibly difficult, we also excluded Iraq and Afghanistan. This selection algorithm left us with 29 cases, and we completed detailed case studies of all 29.

---

[3] We identified spending thresholds through a process of trial and error conducted in concert with our sponsor. We considered the number of cases that would be included by using a number of different investment thresholds ($5 million, $10 million, $20 million, $25 million, and $50 million). Ultimately, we chose the $5 million/$25 million threshold because it got us closest to our project resource–based target of 30 case studies.

Phasing

Twenty years is a long time, and a lot can and does change over such a span. Given that our goal was to assess BPC inputs and outputs in the context of each case, we could not use a single row of data for each case; too many of the input, output, and contextual factors would have changed over time. However, preliminary inquiries did not suggest that we needed to evaluate all factors for all cases on an annual basis. Most factors remained relatively consistent over time, changing only in response to some kind of major shift. Major shifts include exogenous events (such as a regional war or other conflict or 9/11), changes in U.S. priorities, or changes (or crises) inside the PN or the PN's government. Each case was thus broken up into between two and four phases, each representing a row in the project database. The length of each phase was determined holistically at the discretion of the individual case analyst. Phase changes do not reflect small-scale changes or changes on a single factor; rather, they indicate significant shifts and events affecting many factors (or perhaps a smaller number of particularly important factors) in the overall case.

Figure 4.1 shows the phases for each case country in anonymous case rows, along with the rough level of funding across each phase.[4]

---

[4] Given the lack of comprehensive or consistent data on BPC funding, we pulled information from various sources (cross-checking as much as possible for consistency and relying on the most frequently cited sources). Most funding data were drawn from the DoS and DoD *Foreign Military Training and DoD Engagement Activities of Interest* series (1999–2009), the annual USAID Greenbook (U.S. Agency for International Development, *U.S. Overseas Loans and Grants, Obligations, and Loan Authorizations*, Washington, D.C., various years), or the DSCA *Historical Facts Book* (Defense Security Cooperation Agency, *Historical Facts Book*, Washington, D.C., various years). We also used DoD, Congressional Research Service, and U.S. Government Accountability Office reports that focused on particular programs (see Chapter Two) or types of funding. We brought these data sources together in the following ways:

- We captured all DoD-related funding provided through foreign military training, which would include such programs as IMET, regional centers, service academies, Global Peace Operations Initiative (peacekeeping), the Combating Terrorism Fellowship Program, Joint Combined Exercise Training, and unified command exercises.
- We also added "Section 1206"–funded programs and specialized training programs that are unique to specific countries, such as the Counterinsurgency Capability Fund

Figure 4.1
Rough Level of BPC Funding, by Phase

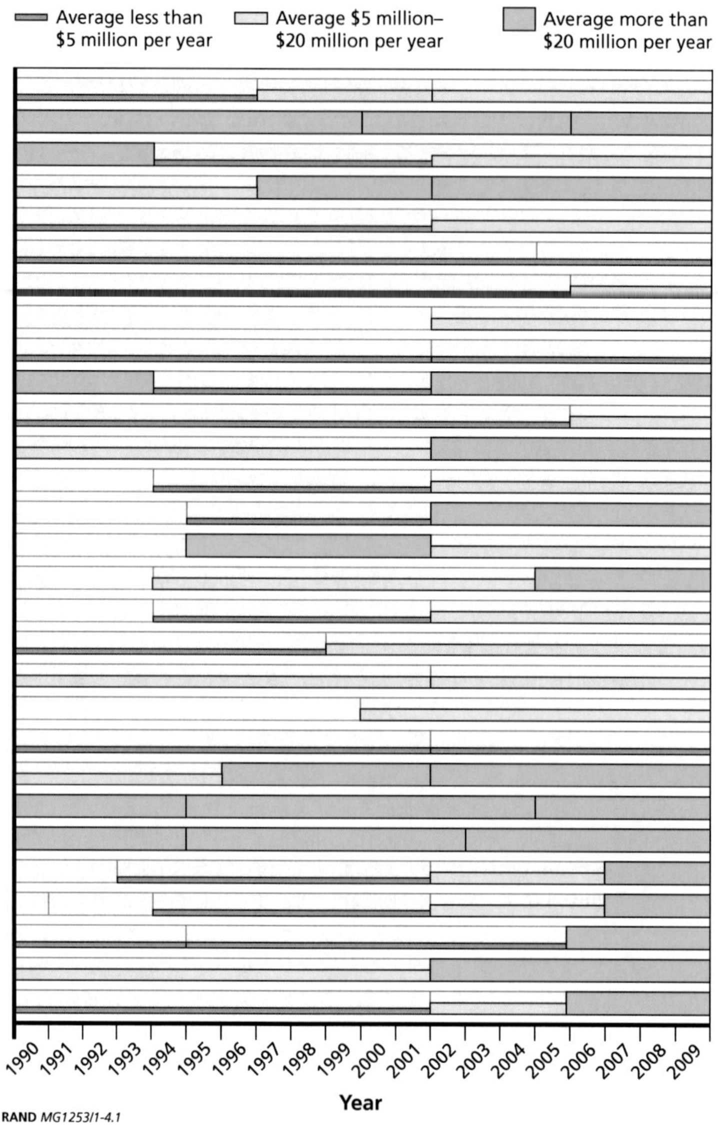

RAND *MG1253/1-4.1*

The thin funding bar indicates that the country received less than $5 million in BPC support per year, on average, during that phase; the medium bar indicates the country received an average of between $5 million and $20 million per year, and the thickest bar indicates that the country received an average of more than $20 million per year during the phase.

Note that several country cases begin with a "null" phase, with no funding indicator bar. We designated phases in which BPC efforts were wholly absent, negligible (perhaps IMET only), or so minimal that we could discern no primary BPC objective as being null phases. We treated these phases as extended baseline phases from which we assessed all characteristics of the subsequent phases.

Data Collection

Each case was the sole responsibility of an individual case analyst. Some data were collected from common sources to ensure comparability, including BPC funding data, population data, geographic data, economic data, and World Bank Governance Indicator data. Where a factor could not be identified in a global database (as was the case for the majority of factors), it was incumbent on the case analyst to ferret out the data. Sources included newspapers (English- and foreign-

---

in Pakistan and counternarcotics programs in Colombia. (The name of the Global Train and Equip "1206" Program refers to Section 1206 in the National Defense Authorization Act for FY 2006, which authorizes the Secretary of Defense, in cooperation with the Secretary of State, to spend up to $350 million each year to build partner counterterrorism and military capacity in support of operations in which the United States is involved.)

- We then included the value of military equipment transferred through drawdowns and the Excess Defense Articles Program.
- Finally, we captured all money spent on military equipment and training through the FMF, FMS and DCS. We calculated the FMS and DCS net of FMF to separate out the partners' contributions to funding U.S. train and equip programs.

In addition, we included a rough calculation of the funds spent on BPC activities by DoS and other agencies through such programs as International Narcotics Control and Law Enforcement and NADR.

language), reports and white papers, other scholarly products, and interviews. Every case was supported by at least one interview. Interview respondents included current and former country directors, division chiefs, desk officers, and action officers (either in relevant staffs at the geographic COCOMs or in OSD), as well as COCOM command historians, PN personnel, and other relevant subject-matter experts.

The resulting case studies capture data at several different analytic levels. At the core of each is all the information that the case analyst was able to collect, along with his or her understanding of the case. This core of information forms the foundation for the data presented and used here. Based on each core case study, the case analysts undertook two case-study treatments: first, scoring all the factors representing all the hypotheses discussed in Chapter Three and, second, preparing a case narrative. Both treatments relied on the same underlying foundation of data, but they do not necessarily connect. Case analysts did *not* compile the case narrative first and then draw factor data exclusively from that narrative, nor did they score all quantitative factors first and then repeat them in prose form for the narrative. The case narratives and the quantitative data are related, but they are not wholly duplicative.

The quantitative data include modified DSART scores for relevant BPC objectives in each phase. Chapter Two described the modified DSART framework, and Chapter Five includes a worked example of DSART scoring, describing how subordinate factors are aggregated and the information and evidence that informed those scorings. See the section "BPC Outcomes in the Analyses" in Chapter Five.

Challenges Overcome in Collecting and Analyzing BPC Data

As the discussion in Chapter Two implied, BPC is a difficult area for analysis. BPC efforts include a wide range of programs and activities, with complex authorities, a multitude of funding sources, and a host of entities and organizations potentially involved in some aspect of planning, oversight, or execution. Records are kept, but usually only by the individual offices or commands with a direct relationship to a program or activity, and not in any centralized or easily accessible repository.

This complexity makes the identification of desired data challenging, let alone the actual collection of those data.

Setting the complexity of inputs and relevant organizations aside, BPC outcomes are challenging. As noted in Chapter Two, BPC can be used to pursue a variety of objectives and purposes. While we reduce this field of objectives to five primary categories of capacity (and the single trump of relationship building), that still leaves considerable variation. Further complicating matters is the difficulty of disentangling BPC efforts when multiple objectives are pursued simultaneously (say, improving border security *and* developing specialty forces for internal use). A second (and related) challenge is disentangling causal conflation. (Was an observed improvement in capacity a result of U.S. BPC efforts, or was it a result of French BPC efforts or the natural product of the partner's own efforts at self-improvement?) A third challenge of this type of analysis concerns the difficulty of observing or measuring capacity or capability that may or may not have actually been used (and all the attendant difficulties of measuring potential).

Finally, there are challenges associated with moving from general information about BPC to information about BPC in specific cases. Chief among them is sensitivity. Not only are data scattered across a range of executing and overseeing organizations and commands, but many of these data are sensitive and could cause embarrassment to either the United States or the specific case partner if disseminated incautiously. Many of these data are not classified (where handling and dissemination controls are clear) but are simply sensitive, and many interview respondents emphasized the importance of protecting that sensitivity. Because of these sensitivities, and because some of the information included in some of the case narratives is classified, the full case narratives appear only in the restricted version of this report.

CHAPTER FIVE

Analyses and Results

This chapter presents our analyses of the 29 country cases whose selection was described in Chapter Four. This chapter begins with a description of the data and the various subsamples of the phases and cases considered in the analyses. This is followed by a discussion of the ways in which changes in DSART scores for different BPC objective areas in different phases were used as analytic outcomes, followed by the analyses and results. The latter sections first address the tests of the various hypotheses (as listed in Chapter Three), then explore patterns of factors and their relationships with outcomes using qualitative comparative analysis. Finally we present our observations from the holistic narratives and other analytic results.

The Data

As discussed in Chapter Four, each of the 29 cases studied was divided into between two and four phases. The average length of a phase is eight years, though some are shorter or longer. In addition to actual case phases (shown in Figure 4.1 in Chapter Four), each case has a baseline phase for which we recorded the baseline DSART scores for BPC objectives that are relevant to the case. These baseline phases report Cold War–era data for many cases, but if a country case begins with a null phase, the baseline would be the DSART scores for that null phase. Taken together, the numbered "actual" phases, the null phases, and the baseline phases total 100.

Each of these 100 phases is represented by a row in the database. For each phase except the baselines, we assigned a score for each of the factors and variables mentioned in relation to the project hypotheses listed in Chapter Three and the DSART scores for relevant BPC objectives. These scores are "1" or "0" (present or absent) for each binary factor, or the actual category or number for categorical or continuous variables. For the baseline phases, we recorded only the baseline DSART scores. For each non-baseline phase, the data rows include scores for roughly 75 factors.

Of the 100 phases, 38 are null or baseline phases, and 62 are "real," numbered phases in which the United States conducted BPC activities with discernable intent. In 55 of those 62 phases, at least one of the primary BPC objectives was a form of BPC—that is, relationship building or access was not the only primary objective, and efforts really did include some kind of attempt to build actual capacity. (In the other seven phases, relationship building was the only discernable objective).[1] These 55 phases in which capacity building was a goal, then, constitute the analytic core of all the analyses seeking to discern the effectiveness of different BPC efforts in different contexts in actually building capacity. However, the hypothesis designated H1b asserts that where relationship building or access is a primary objective, capacity outcomes may not correlate well with expenditures or effort. In anticipation of H1b receiving empirical support (which it does), we further refined the data subsets to recognize that cases in which building relationships or securing access is also a primary objective may not fairly represent effective practices or contextual factors, as some of the effort is being spent on relationships and not wholly on capacity building. A total of 22 phases have relationship building or access as a primary objective; this set includes the seven phases noted previously, in which relationship building or access is the only primary objective, as

---

[1] Note that improving relations with a PN is always a goal to some degree; it is the foundation of foreign policy and an important contributor to effective capacity building. For relationship building or access to be a primary goal of BPC, however, it needed to have been equal to or more of a priority than actual capacity building. That is, relationship building or access was scored as a primary objective only when it was clearly the highest-priority foreign policy goal.

well as 15 phases in which some sort of capacity building is a primary objective but relationship building or access is also a primary objective. Considering the 55 phases in which capacity building is an objective and removing phases in which relationship building or access is *also* an objective leaves a data subset of 40. These 40 phases represent "pure" efforts to build capacity. Figure 5.1 presents a Venn diagram of the various subsets of the phases.

In addition to the multiple phases and factors scored for the 29 cases, each case study includes a detailed holistic case narrative. The narrative data for the case studies are an important part of the overall analytic scheme, offering additional confirmation, understanding, and nuance that the quantified data do not always provide.

Figure 5.1
Venn Diagram of the Subsets of Phases in the Data

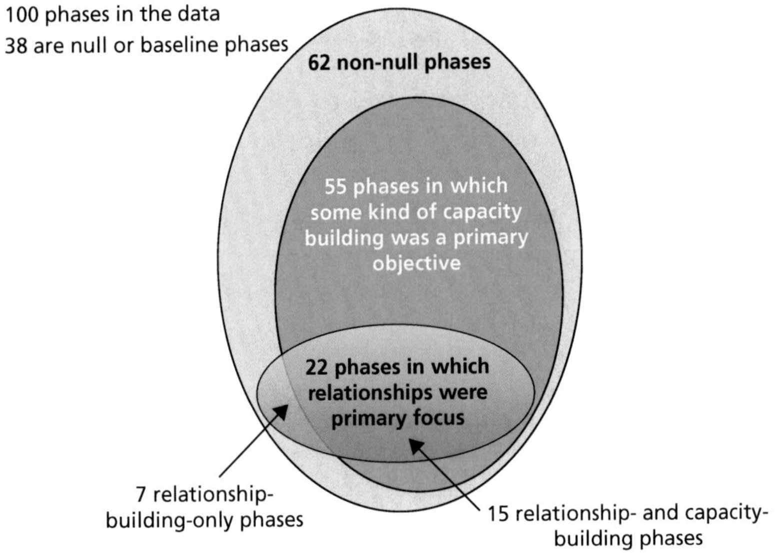

RAND *MG1253/1-5.1*

BPC Outcomes in the Analyses

As noted earlier, measuring outcomes for efforts to build partner capacity is challenging. We elected to resolve this challenge by using the modified DSART scoring scheme described in Chapter Two to assess partner capacity in each of the five BPC objective areas also identified in that chapter. This provided us with a score, ranging from 1 to 5, for the relevant BPC objectives in each case phase and for the case baseline. In this section, we present a worked example from one of the case studies, interspersed with clarifying discussion.

Worked Example: Identifying the Primary BPC Objectives

In one of the phases of one of the case-study countries, we identified two primary BPC objectives: internal security and border or maritime security. We identified these specific objectives after a thorough review of the vast unclassified literature on U.S. capacity-building efforts in the country, as well as several interviews with subject-matter experts on internal security in the country and on U.S. assistance to the country.

Worked Example: Listing the DSART Subcategories for the Objective

The DSART subcategories for internal security are as follows:

- Ability to train military forces for counterterrorism, counterinsurgency, or counternarcotics operations
- Ability to carry out surveillance, reconnaissance, and intelligence operations
- Ability to maintain security throughout the country, including protection of critical infrastructure; ability to prevent terrorist/insurgent attacks
- Sufficient ministerial capacity to plan and integrate strategy and operations
- Ability to combat corruption
- Ability to police, prosecute, and incarcerate drug traffickers, terrorists, and insurgents
- Ability to deploy rapid and mobile reaction capabilities

- Logistics for, and maintenance and sustainment of, these capabilities
- Ability to establish drug eradication and interdiction programs (conditional).

Worked Example: Scoring the DSART Subcategories and Noting Changes

Each of the DSART subcategories is scored on the following scale (as presented in Chapter Two):

1. *very low:* entirely lacking
2. *low:* beginning to develop
3. *neither low nor high:* minimal but functioning
4. *high:* functional but room for improvement
5. *very high:* strong and no major improvement needed.

For the example phase of the example case, each subcategory of internal security is scored as follows.

Ability to train military forces for counterterrorism, counterinsurgency, or counternarcotics operations

Previous phase baseline score: 4; new phase score: 5

These scores were based on holistic assessments drawing on several sources that directly or indirectly provided information about the ability of the country's special forces to train other forces for counterterrorism, counterinsurgency, and counternarcotics operations. Between a previous phase and the phase of interest, PN capabilities to conduct this type of training improved from functional with room for improvement to strong, with no major improvement needed. By the end of the phase, U.S. advisers considered PN special forces to be at the same qualitative level as U.S. special forces.

Ability to carry out surveillance, reconnaissance, and intelligence operations

Previous phase baseline score: 3; new phase score: 4

A holistic assessment based on data from anonymous subject-matter expert interviews, as well as open-source literature that documented the planning advice and training provided by U.S. special forces to PN security force personnel in the area of intelligence fusion, led to these scores. Throughout the phase, special forces training was partly responsible for the increased ability of PN counterinsurgency forces to conduct intelligence, surveillance, and reconnaissance operations, which improved from minimal but functioning in the previous phase to functional with room for improvement in the phase of interest.

Ability to maintain security throughout the country, including protection of critical infrastructure; ability to prevent terrorist/insurgent attacks

Previous phase baseline score: 3; new phase score: 3

There was no score change; the data showed that the ability of PN security forces to maintain security throughout the country—including the ability to protect critical infrastructure and prevent terrorist or insurgent attacks—remained at the level of minimal but functioning. Several of those interviewed acknowledged that even with increased air mobility, the terrain still posed a major challenge to PN security forces.

Sufficient ministerial capacity to plan and integrate strategy and operations

Previous phase baseline score: 3; new phase score: 4

Scores were based on a holistic assessment drawing on several sources that directly or indirectly provided information about U.S. efforts in this area, which included providing assistance to the police to build new stations and offering Roving Base Defense Course training. Another capability leveraged for the PN rural police program was the U.S. military psychological support and civil affairs teams, which contributed through a focus on winning the support of the local population. By the end of the phase, U.S. BPC efforts resulted in the ability of PN forces to plan and integrate strategy and operations, which improved from minimal but functioning to functional with room for improvement.

Ability to combat corruption

Previous phase baseline score: 3; new phase score: 3

There was no score change; the ability of the PN government and security forces to combat corruption continued to function at the level of minimal but functioning. While the government did make substantial progress in improving its ability to counter corruption from the beginning of an even earlier phase to the end of the phase of interest (from beginning to develop to minimal but functioning), developing a robust capability in this area takes years, if not decades.

Ability to police, prosecute, and incarcerate drug traffickers, terrorists, and insurgents

Previous phase baseline score 3; new phase score: 3

There was no score change; the ability of the PN government and security forces to police, prosecute, and incarcerate drug traffickers, terrorists, and insurgents largely remained at the level of minimal but functioning. In this case, this subcategory is closely related to the ability of the PN government to combat corruption.

Ability to deploy rapid and mobile reaction capabilities

Previous phase baseline score: 4; new phase score: 4

No score change was recorded, primarily because the PN's ability to deploy rapid and mobile reaction capabilities had already improved significantly throughout the previous phase, leaving little room for improvement during the phase of interest. High-functioning rapid and mobile reaction capabilities were evident during a joint exercise. Following years of U.S. special forces training, improvements were clear in the available documentary evidence. Improved airlift capabilities could bring PN counterinsurgency forces closer to the area of conflict. An improved logistics and sustainment capability meant that PN soldiers could stay in the jungles for longer periods. Furthermore, helicopters provided as part of BPC efforts drastically improved the mobility of PN forces, significantly enhanced the firepower of PN security forces, and leveled the playing field against the insurgents.

Logistics for, and maintenance and sustainment of, these capabilities

Previous phase baseline score: 3; new phase score: 4

A holistic assessment based on several sources that directly or indirectly provided information about maintenance and sustainment efforts that began during the previous phase and took hold during the phase of interest contributed to identifying this capability improvement. Around the same time, DoS and DoD initiated programs to train PN army pilots, crew chiefs, and mechanics so that the army could fly and maintain the provided helicopters.

Ability to establish drug eradication and interdiction programs (conditional)

Previous phase baseline score: 4; new phase score: 4

This conditional subcategory was scored for this case because counter-narcotics initiatives were highly relevant to this particular PN's internal security mission area. There was no score change; the ability of the PN government and security forces to establish drug eradication and interdiction programs remained at the level of functional but room for improvement. While counternarcotics remained a critical part of PN internal security efforts during this phase, the emphasis on counterinsurgency operations meant that drug eradication and interdiction programs were not always the top priority.

Worked Example: Calculating BPC Outcomes

Effectiveness in BPC must be about improving capacity, so we are looking for improvement from phase to phase, or from baseline to phase.

In the worked example case, the previous phase baseline DSART score for internal security was 4 + 3 + 3 + 3 + 3 + 3 + 4 + 3 + 4, divided by 9 (the number of subcategories), for a score of 3.33. The DSART score for internal security for the new phase was 5 + 4 + 3 + 4 + 3 + 3 + 4 + 4 + 4 ÷ 9 = 3.77.

Two questions remain: How much improvement constitutes effectiveness, and how exactly should different outcome measures be assessed?

Our raw outcome is the delta (change) in the DSART score for a BPC objective area from phase to phase. In this example, the baseline composite DSART score for BPC objective category 1, internal security, for the previous phase was 3.33, and the new phase's DSART score for that objective category was 3.77. The delta DSART was 0.44. In some respects, that calculation of raw delta DSART is sufficient as an outcome measure. Factors that are associated with larger improvements on the DSART are presumed to be more effective. Three issues, however, led us to use adjusted DSART-based outcomes:

- phases with multiple BPC objectives
- the relative difficulty of improving on high DSART scores compared with lower scores
- the fact that several of the analyses we conducted prefer binary (0,1) outcomes.

Next, we describe each issue and how we resolved it.

Phases with multiple BPC objectives occurred frequently in the data. Of the 55 phases that included at least one BPC objective as primary, 30 included more than one primary BPC objective. The case in our worked example is an example of this, with both internal security and border/maritime security as primary objectives in the phase of interest. We resolved this issue by averaging the delta of DSART scores between phases. Thus, if a phase showed a delta DSART score of 0.44 for internal security (BPC objective category 1) and a delta DSART score of 0.80 for border/maritime forces (BPC objective category 5), then the average delta DSART score would be 0.62. We chose to average rather than add multiple DSART objectives because many of our factors are characteristic rather than cumulative. For example, if the factors of greatest interest are money invested and total exercises conducted, then it might be reasonable to add delta DSART scores to reflect that equal deltas in two objective categories may well have taken twice as much funding or twice as many exercises. However, when the factors of greatest interest are characteristics or properties of the BPC effort or the country—for example, whether or not the major BPC activities included sustainment components or whether or not U.S. and PN interests aligned—we would expect them to affect all BPC efforts and not be consumed by or allocated specifically to one BPC objective or the other. If U.S. and PN interests align in a phase and that is correlated with effectiveness, we do not want the outcome to be doubled simply because the BPC effort targeted two objectives in that phase.

We make the (quite reasonable) assumption that it is easier to go from nothing to something than from something to something better. That is, *moving from low DSART scores to middle DSART scores is easier (and less costly) than moving from middle DSART scores to high ones.* Clearly, progressing from a DSART score of "1" (entirely lacking) to a DSART score of "2" (beginning to develop) is a much more modest achievement than moving from a DSART score of "4" (functional but room for improvement) to a DSART score of "5" (strong and no major improvements needed). Using just the average delta DSART score for an outcome would require two assumptions: first, that DSART scores for different BPC objectives are on the same scale and have the same meaning and, second, that the DSART scale has consistent units—that is, changes in the DSART scale (for example, the difference between 2 and 3 and between 3 and 4) are of equal intervals. The first assumption is relatively reasonable; the 1–5 DSART scale is applied to all supporting capabilities for all five BPC objectives in the same way. The second assumption, however, contradicts the earlier assumption about ease of improvement and thus requires some kind of remediation. Based on our assumption that higher DSART scores are harder to improve upon, we decided to weight delta DSART scores accordingly. The weighting scheme we adopted is simple: A score's weight is determined by the DSART score baseline for that phase.

In our worked example, the DSART score for BPC objective 1 (internal security) at the end of the previous phase was 3.33, and at the end of the new phase it was 3.77. As noted earlier, the raw delta DSART score was 0.44. Taking into account the relatively high baseline capability in the previous phase, when weighted, that delta becomes 0.44 × 3.33, or 1.47. This still does not answer the question: How much change constitutes effectiveness?

Several of the analyses we conducted prefer binary (0,1) outcomes, so we needed to translate the delta DSART scores that were based on continuous outcomes. Transforming a continuous parameter into a binary parameter is relatively simple, conceptually: One simply identifies a threshold and declares values below the threshold to be "absent" (0) and values above the threshold to be present (1). While easy to understand, actually choosing a good threshold can be tricky. To transform the weighted delta DSART score for a phase into a binary variable for indicating effectiveness, we examined the distribution of the score across all phases of all cases. Ideally, when looking for a threshold, one hopes that a quantitative graph, such as a histogram, will have one or more separate and distinct "humps" and that the threshold can be placed between the humps, dividing the parameter based on an observable empirical cut point that is obvious in the raw data. While there were peaks and valleys in the distribution of the weighted delta DSART scores in our example, they were not so unambiguous as to allow a definitive empirically derived cut point, as shown in Figure 5.2.

To include additional information upon which to base the threshold decision for a binary BPC effectiveness outcome measure, each case analyst was asked to assess BPC effectiveness in each phase of each case in a single subjective holistic score: 0 if the capacity built was negligible, 1 if capacity built/overall degree of success was modest or low, 2 if overall success was decent or good, and 3 if overall success was strong or excellent. Using these assessments led us to use 0.8 as the threshold, which corresponds to a valley in the histogram of weighted average delta DSART scores, and also accounts for 53 of 55 of the case analysts' assessments. (Two phases were identified as resulting in low capacity built, exceeding the threshold; thus, they were considered "effective" in the binary analyses.) In our worked example, the weighted delta DSART of 1.47 is well above the threshold for "effective," which aligns with what the case narrative indicates.

Figure 5.2
Histogram of Weighted Average Delta DSART Scores

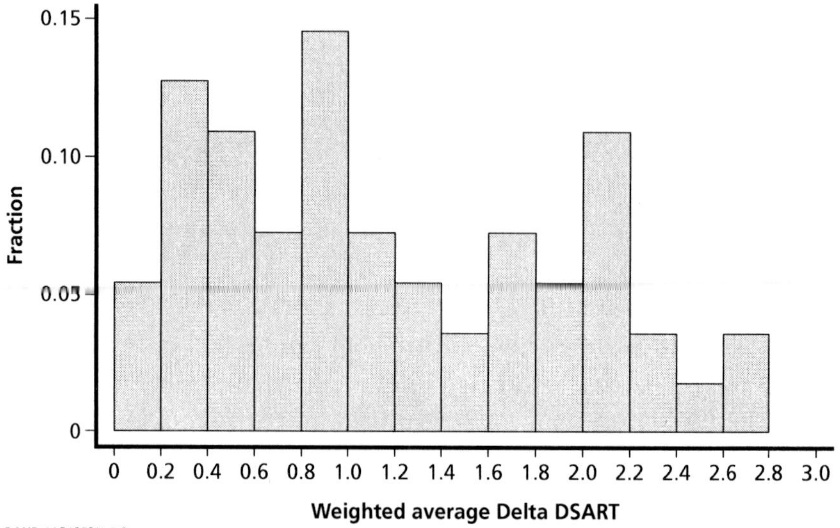

RAND *MG1253/1-5.2*

For all quantitative analyses that consider the effectiveness of capacity building in a phase, we used the *weighted delta DSART score* if a continuous outcome is appropriate, and assessed *binary effectiveness* where a binary outcome was called for, with both constructed as described here.

Testing the Hypotheses

Chapter Three presented the project hypotheses and listed the factors that represent those hypotheses in the data. In this chapter, we test the hypotheses. The core test of hypotheses presented in this report is simple bivariate correlation. If a hypothesis is represented by a scaled or continuous factor, then we calculate the correlation between that factor and the weighted delta DSART score. If a hypothesis is represented by a binary factor, we calculate the correlation between that factor and binary effectiveness. In general, if we find a correlation coefficient of 0.4 or greater, we report strong support for the hypothesis; a correlation between 0.15 and 0.4 equates to modest support; correlations between 0.05 and 0.15 indicate minimal support, and correlations below 0.05 or that run in the direction opposite the hypothesized direction (negative) mean that the hypothesis has no support. In addition to correlation-based assessment of the hypotheses, we include evidence from the narrative results. For example, if a factor provides only a modest correlation but is strongly confirmed at the narrative level or perfectly predicts one outcome or the other through its presence or absence, we upgrade the level of support claimed accordingly.

Hypothesis Test Results

This section presents the results from our tests of the project hypotheses. Hypotheses are listed in the same order in which they were presented in Chapter Three.

Parent hypothesis 1: The ways in which the United States plans, resources, and executes BPC influences effectiveness.

H1a: The more money you spend, the more partner capacity you build.

While offered as a straw man, *H1a receives strong support*. As with many expenditure relationships, the relationship is not linear—that is, there is not a one-to-one correspondence between additional dollars and additional capacity, returns diminish. The log transformation removed the curve from the relationship between expenditures and capacity building. The correlation between the log of $ millions spent on BPC and weighted delta DSART scores over all 55 phases in which some form of capacity building was a primary objective was 0.48. Considering only the 40 cases in which capacity building was the only primary objective (the non-relationship cases), the correlation goes up to 0.68, one of the strongest relationships reported here.

H1b: Where relationship building/access is a primary objective, capacity outcomes may not correlate well with expenditures/efforts.

We know from the case narratives that in some cases in which building relationships is one of the primary objectives, some fraction of increased spending serves to "buy friends" rather than buy capacity.

What we observed in the narratives is borne out by the quantitative data in the noticeable increase in the correlation between expenditures and BPC effectiveness when we exclude phases that include relationship building as a primary objective. To further test H1b, we calculated the correlation between the log of expenditures and BPC effectiveness in the 15 phases that include both relationship building or access *and* some form of capacity building as primary objectives. That correlation is 0.07, a very minimal level of association. *H1b receives strong support.*

H1c: . . . and that is OK.

It is not surprising that when "buying friends" joins "buying capacity" as an objective, that investment correlates less strongly with capacity built. In the phases in which relationship building and some form of capacity building were both primary objectives, positive or better relationships were maintained, or relationships improved to positive or better in 13 of the 15 phases.

H1d: Consistency produces better results; stable, designated resources improve the likelihood of reaching objectives.

Inconsistency clearly correlates with low effectiveness. Inconsistent funding has a correlation of –0.41 with binary effectiveness, and disjoint delivery correlates at a level of –0.35. This, coupled with narrative evidence of the importance of consistency, constitutes *strong support for H1d.*

H1e: Incorporating sustainment considerations into the effort increases the likelihood of the partner retaining the capability.

The correlation between inclusion of a sustainment component in BPC and its (binary) effectiveness is 0.49. This offers *strong support for H1e,* support that is echoed in the individual case narratives.[2]

H1f: Temporary punitive funding decrements have modest adverse consequences for BPC efforts.

The correlation between a temporary punitive funding break and binary effectiveness is a paltry –0.07. However, narrative findings support the notion that these punitive breaks do slow BPC, just not so much that some progress in capacity building is not still made over the course of a lengthy phase. This adds up to *minimal support for H1f.*

H1g: Long-term punitive funding decrements have lasting adverse consequences for partner capacity.

The correlation between a major punitive disruption and binary effectiveness is –0.05. Again, the narrative findings note that punitive breaks always adversely affect capacity building, but perhaps less adversely than one might imagine. There are two mitigating factors: the recovery time available in longer phases and the fact that punitive funding interruptions do not always interrupt all funding or all delivery. This produces the barest minimum of *minimal support for H1g.*

H1h: Punitive funding decrements can provide leverage and improve behaviors that resulted in the funding cut.

Punitive funding cuts appear to slow BPC effectiveness, but they do not have the devastating consequences that proponents of H1f and H1g might expect. Furthermore, these punitive funding cuts do correlate with improved behavior on the part of the PN. Specifically, of the ten

---

[2] A reviewer asked what our results suggested about how long the United States should plan to provide sustainment funding and when it could expect to transition sustainment to the partner. Our quantitative analyses were not designed to answer this interesting question. Considering the case narratives holistically, the answer is "it depends." One of the narrative-level findings discussed later in this chapter notes that BPC takes time, and a variety of different factors drive the time it takes. We expect similar variation when predicting how long is "long enough" for U.S.-funded sustainment. This remains an interesting topic for future research.

phases that included a punitive funding reduction, four saw significant improvement in the behavior that led to the punishment. Of the four phases in which *lengthy* punitive funding decrements occurred, three resulted in significant improvement. Thus, we have correlations of 0.03 and 0.5, respectively. This offers *moderate support for H1b*, which might be stronger if the hypothesis were modified to consider only lengthy substantial funding decrements.

Parent hypothesis 2: You can lead a horse to water but you cannot make it drink: Low partner motivation is adverse to capacity outcomes

H2a: Differences between U.S. and PN BPC goals reduce effectiveness.

The correlation between the factor "PN BPC goals/desires differ substantially from U.S. goals" and binary effectiveness is –0.4, amounting to *strong support for H2a*.

H2b: BPC efforts are more successful when U.S. and PN strategic aims align/when BPC efforts address areas of mutual concern.

The correlation between binary effectiveness and the constructed factor "Strategic interests align *and* the BPC effort targets an area of mutual concern" is 0.46. Considering only phases in which relationship building was not a primary objective, this correlation goes up to 0.56. Either correlation is sufficient to offer *strong support for H2b*.

Examples of this correlation abound. For example, in Mexico, approximately 3,200 personnel were trained by U.S. special forces trainers in rapid response operations between 1996 and 1999. During this same time period, the number of Mexican airmen trained at the Inter-American Air Forces Academy at Lackland Air Force Base, Texas, increased from 141 to 331. It was around 1998 that both Mexico and the United States began forming a shared understanding of the severity of the threat in Mexico. This shared understanding led to overall more effective efforts to work together on a range of issues, especially counternarcotics.

H2c: Capacity built to meet PN objectives is more likely to be sustained/used by the partner.

H2c receives strong support from a correlation of 0.45 between binary BPC effectiveness and the factor "Capability built clearly aligns with PN objectives." All seven phases in which BPC efforts did not clearly align with PN objectives did not meet the threshold for binary effectiveness.

H2d: Partners that invest their own funds to maintain capability, conduct training, or invest in maintenance programs will have more success.

The correlation between binary effectiveness and partners making a substantial investment in developing or maintaining capabilities is 0.56. Considering only the 40 phases in which relationship building was not a primary objective, that correlation goes up to 0.63, one of the highest cited in this report. This amounts to *strong support for H2d.* Of the 18 phases in which the PN did not make a substantial investment in the BPC capability, only three met the threshold for binary effectiveness.

H2e: BPC efforts with a PN with a demonstrated commitment to national defense are more effective.

Neither raw defense spending nor defense spending as a fraction of GDP is correlated with the weighted delta DSART score. On reflection, PN defense spending, while a good indication of PN commitment to defense overall, is not necessarily an indicator of commitment to BPC; after all, we do not know how much of this annual defense spending goes toward areas targeted by BPC. As the hypothesis is stated, this amounts to *no support for H2e.*

H2f: Effective capacity building leads to effective relationship building.

The correlation between a PN having a good (as opposed to a poor or adequate) relationship with the United States and binary effectiveness is 0.46. The correlation between improvement in a partner's relationship with the United States during a phase and binary effectiveness is 0.22, but "improvement" does not take into account whether the initial relationship was poor or quite good, which could affect the association. These correlations amount to *strong support for H2f.* However, the narrative results suggest that a caveat be added to the hypothesis: . . . *or vice versa*. Many phases of many cases show relationships and capacity improving in tandem, with some cases showing BPC efforts breaking the ice and leading to improved relationships and others showing improved relationships better enabling collaboration to build capacity. The strong correlation between the two does not require that one always precede the other. Both the quantitative data and the narratives suggest that good relationships and effective BPC go hand in hand.

Parent hypothesis 3: PN baseline capabilities (in government, economy, and defense) influence the effectiveness of BPC.

H3a: Willing but otherwise unprepared partners have lower absorptive capacity, limiting the effectiveness of BPC.

H3a receives strong support, with a correlation of –0.49 between partners with low absorptive capacity and binary effectiveness. Thirteen of the 16 phases in which a PN's absorptive capacity was scored as low produced delta DSART scores that did not meet the threshold for binary effectiveness.

H3b: Activities matched to partner baseline capabilities and absorptive capacity increase the effectiveness of BPC efforts.

Fortunately, a significant mismatch between PN baseline or absorptive capacity and the level and type of U.S. BPC activities occurred only six times in the 55 core phases. In four of those six phases, the threshold for binary effectiveness was not achieved, providing a correlation of –0.16. The narrative accounts, however, suggest that such mismatches *always* resulted in reduced effectiveness but that in some phases, initial mismatches were sufficiently corrected or overcome by the end of a phase to produce effective BPC outcomes anyway. Based on both the quantitative and narrative analysis, we find *moderate support for H3b.*

H3c: BPC efforts are more effective with democratic partners who have relatively positive governance indicators.

The correlation between a PN's World Bank Governance Indicator percentile rank and weighted delta DSART score is 0.46. Unsurprisingly, this relationship depends to a great extent on whether or not building relationships is a primary BPC objective. If building relationships is not a primary objective, the correlation goes up to a prodigious 0.57. This provides *strong support for H3c regarding governance.*

In phases where relationship building or access is a primary goal, the correlation is –0.06 (effectively 0). This is no doubt reflective of the fact that the primacy of relationships comes at the expense of actual capacity building (as discussed earlier), as well as the fact that some of the countries with which the United States seeks improved relationships or from which it wishes to secure access are not always particularly well governed.

The data provide only *moderate support for H3c regarding democratization.* While seven out of eight phases taking place in a mature democracy met the threshold for binary BPC effectiveness, partial democracies statistically did no better than non-democracies. This is unsurprising, as other RAND research has shown partial or transitional democracies to be at greater risk or more vulnerable in other respects.[3]

H3d: Disputed leadership leads to worse outcomes.

The data offer *moderate support for H3d,* with a correlation of –0.16 between disputed leadership and binary effectiveness. The narrative evidence indicates that all phases with leadership disputes resulted in much lower BPC effectiveness than would have been the case otherwise.

---

[3] Christopher Paul, Russell W. Glenn, Beth Grill, Megan P. McKernan, Barbara Raymond, Matt Stafford, and Horacio R. Trujillo, "Identifying Urban Flashpoints: A Delphi Derived Model for Scoring Cities' Vulnerability to Large Scale Unrest," *Studies in Conflict and Terrorism,* Vol. 31, No. 11, 2008.

H3e: BPC will be more effective with partners that have reasonably strong/healthy economies.

The correlation between a PN's Human Development Index percentile (which, it should be noted, measures more than just a country's economy) and weighted delta DSART score is 0.34, which amounts to *moderate support for H3e.*[4]

Parent hypothesis 4: The broader context (the geopolitical situation, other neighbors and partners) influences the effectiveness of BPC.

H4a:* Allegro non troppo: *The United States wants some partners to gain capacity—but not too much capacity—for a regional balance of power; when this is the case, outcomes may be capped relative to inputs.

The correlation between the presence of the factor "Practical limit on the amount of capacity that the United States desires to build" and binary effectiveness is –0.33, showing *moderate support for H4a*. Interestingly, at the narrative level, such constraints appear more likely to affect the relationship with the PN than the capacity developed. Of course, an adverse impact on relationships can have an adverse impact on the effectiveness of capacity building.[5]

---

[4] A reviewer noted that "presumably, the relationship between BPC effectiveness and economic strength is not linear." We agree. The relationship between a country's Human Development Index percentile and weighted delta DSART score was fairly linear in our analysis, but both are in units that are not easily interpreted. (The Human Development Index is a composite index with a threshold of 1 to 100; the units of the weighted delta DSART scores are difficult to interpret beyond greater or lesser improvement in the modified DSART functions.) It would be useful to know "where the bends are" in the nonlinear relationship between a PN's economy and BPC effectiveness in order to know whether there is a minimum floor for PN economic strength below which certain kinds of BPC are unlikely to work, or if there is a level of economic health that is good enough for most BPC and makes high PN economic strength moot. This remains an interesting question for further research—perhaps research involving multiple measures of economic strength and more specific measures of effectiveness.

[5] For example, "What do you mean you won't sell us/give us __________?"

H4b: BPC efforts of other countries can work at "cross-purposes" with U.S. BPC efforts, either by monopolizing elite troops and resources or by distracting the PN from the desired U.S. focus.

A country that is not a U.S. ally spending more on BPC than the United States in a phase is negatively correlated with binary effectiveness (–0.25, to be precise). All three of the phases in which the case analysts scored "Other country's BPC efforts detracted from U.S. BPC efforts (distracted PN from U.S. objectives, monopolized PN elite troops or resources)" as present did not meet the threshold for effective BPC. This evidence constitutes *moderate support for H4b*. Doubtless, some countries work to develop capacity in complementary ways, with varying effectiveness; however, the BPC efforts of other countries sometimes work at cross-purposes, muddying the waters.

H4c: 9/11 was a watershed that made U.S. BPC more focused; post-9/11 BPC is more effective.

The correlations between post-9/11 phases and binary effectiveness is 0.4; this correlation goes up to 0.52 if we omit phases in which relationship building was a primary objective. This provides *strong support for H4c*. Several things changed with 9/11. First, efforts with existing partners became more focused. While pre-9/11 BPC often sought to improve a PN's defense forces in a generic way (e.g., better equipment, better training), post-9/11 BPC was more focused on specific missions (for example, counterterrorism, counterpiracy, internal security, or support for coalition operations). Second, 9/11 brought a new focus to U.S. national security interests, and, thus, there were some significant changes in the priority accorded to partners. Nations that previously had very modest relationships with the United States rocketed to prominence, with new efforts focused on specific capabilities and with no lengthy history of generic baseline efforts. Third and finally (though by no means of least importance), after 9/11, the overall funds available for BPC were considerably greater. All three of these factors differentiate the pre-9/11 period from the post-9/11 period. While it is tempting to attribute the bulk of the improvements to the increased funding available, the narratives urge a more balanced view.

Post-9/11 Kenya provides an example. There, U.S. BPC efforts benefited from a close alignment between Kenya's own security concerns about terrorist threats emerging from neighboring states and the U.S. objective of countering transnational terrorism in the Horn of Africa. U.S. BPC efforts in Kenya after 9/11 worked because objectives were clear and clearly focused on counterterrorism.

Hypothesis Test Summary

Table 5.1 summarizes the degree of support provided for each project hypothesis.

Table 5.1
Summary of Support for Project Hypotheses

Hypothesis	Description	Degree of Support
H1a	The more money you spend, the more partner capacity you build.	Strong
H1b	Where relationship building/access is a primary objective, capacity outcomes may not correlate well with expenditures/efforts.	Strong
H1c	. . . and that is OK.	NA
H1d	Consistency produces better results; stable, designated resources improve the likelihood of reaching objectives.	Strong
H1e	Incorporating sustainment considerations into the effort increases the likelihood of the partner retaining the capability.	Strong
H1f	Temporary punitive funding decrements have modest adverse consequences for BPC efforts.	Minimal
H1g	Long-term punitive funding decrements have lasting adverse consequences for partner capacity.	Minimal
H1h	Punitive funding decrements can provide leverage and improve behaviors that resulted in the funding cut.	Moderate
H2a	Differences between U.S. and PN BPC goals reduce effectiveness.	Strong

Table 5.1—Continued

Hypothesis	Description	Degree of Support
H2b	BPC efforts are more successful when U.S. and PN strategic aims align/when BPC efforts address areas of mutual concern.	Strong
H2c	Capacity built to meet PN objectives is more likely to be sustained/used by the partner.	Strong
H2d	Partners that invest their own funds to maintain capability, conduct training, or invest in maintenance programs will have more success.	Strong
H2e	BPC efforts with a PN with a demonstrated commitment to national defense are more effective.	No support
H2f	Effective capacity building leads to effective relationship building.	Strong
H3a	Willing but otherwise unprepared partners have lower absorptive capacity, limiting the effectiveness of BPC.	Strong
H3b	Activities matched to partner baseline capabilities and absorptive capacity increase the effectiveness of BPC efforts.	Moderate
H3c	BPC efforts are more effective with democratic partners who have relatively positive governance indicators.	Strong (governance) Moderate (democratization)
H3d	Disputed leadership leads to worse outcomes.	Moderate
H3e	BPC will be more effective with partners that have reasonably strong/healthy economies.	Moderate
H4a	*Allegro non troppo:* The United States wants some partners to gain capacity—but not too much capacity—for a regional balance of power; when this is the case, outcomes may be capped relative to inputs.	Moderate
H4b	BPC efforts of other countries can work at "cross-purposes" with U.S. BPC efforts, either by monopolizing elite troops and resources or by distracting the PN from the desired U.S. focus.	Moderate
H4c	9/11 was a watershed that made U.S. BPC more focused; post-9/11 BPC is more effective.	Strong

Hypotheses, by BPC Objective

H1b asserts that relationship building as an objective is different, and the evidence strongly supports the notion that capacity building is often sacrificed when relationship building is a primary objective. However, Chapter Two identified six different objectives for BPC activities, five of which focus on different forms of capacity. Do the hypotheses work differently when different BPC objectives are pursued? The short answer is, other than when relationship building is a primary BPC objective, not really.

Table 5.2 shows the number of phases that included each of the five core capacity-building objectives. The total is greater than 55, the number of phases considered, because many phases had more than one primary objective.

Unfortunately, the seven cases that included conventional forces as a primary BPC objective are too small a subset from which to draw conclusions, especially considering that five of those seven cases also had relationship building as a primary BPC objective.

The objective categories 1, 3, and 5 have sufficient cases to consider separately. However, many of these cases involved more than one objective from categories 1, 3, and 5, making this separation difficult. Twenty-two of the 48 phases that had a category 1, 3, or 5 primary objective also included at least one objective from the other two categories. Fortunately, building specialty forces for internal use, for external use, or for border security appear to be BPC activities that have more in common than building conventional capacity or building ministe-

Table 5.2
Number of Phases in Which BPC Objective Was Present

Objective Category	Number of Phases
1. Internal security	28
2. Conventional forces	7
3. Specialty forces for external use	17
4. Ministerial capacity	10
5. Border or maritime security	25

rial capacity. Though we were unable to separate the three categories effectively, we were able to consider them in combination.

The data include 38 phases in which the BPC effort sought to meet at least one category 1, 3, or 5 objective but did not also include a primary objective from category 2 or 4.

Reevaluating all project hypotheses using only these 38 phases produces unsurprising results: All hypotheses supported by data from all phases are also supported in the objective category 1-, 3-, and 5-only phases. Further, in many cases, the observed correlations are moderately stronger or larger. This increase in coefficient magnitude does not push any of the hypotheses to a higher level of support, however.

This general finding of stronger correlations for the objective category 1-, 3-, and 5-only phases suggests that most of the exceptions to the project hypotheses occurred in the phases that focused on conventional forces (category 2) or ministerial capacity (category 4).

As is clear in Table 5.2, ministerial capacity was a primary objective in only ten phases. This is a fairly slim empirical foundation from which to generalize, but, with caution, we elected to recalculate all the hypothesis-related correlations for this subsample.

The results were quite interesting. For most hypotheses, the correlations follow those found in all phase analyses, with modest variation up or down and two striking exceptions. First, for all other objectives, low absorptive capacity on the part of the PN correlates with low effectiveness; however, for ministerial capacity building, the correlation is much more modest ($r = 0.49$ for all data, but $r = 0.15$ for category 4). This suggests (and intuition agrees) that ministerial capacity building itself can help improve absorptive capacity and does not require much of a baseline from which to make improvements. Second, while all phases show a strong correlation between BPC effectiveness and positive governance indicators, phases that included ministerial capacity building as a primary objective have an astoundingly high (0.91) correlation between governance indicators and effectiveness, suggesting that it is easier to develop defense ministries in governments that are already effective in other areas and that it is correspondingly harder to do so in countries with otherwise ineffective governments.

Qualitative Comparative Analysis

Thus far, all of our analyses have been bivariate. That is, they have involved only two variables: the outcome for all BPC objectives or a subset thereof (either the weighted delta DSART score or binary effectiveness) and a single factor representing a hypothesis. To what extent do these many different factors occur together or relate to outcomes jointly? This is a multivariate question that we can answer with multivariate analysis.

The most familiar form of multivariate analysis is probably regression. We do not employ regression on these data for several reasons, two of which we discuss here. First, the number of phases of interest (either 55 or 40 in almost all analyses) is on the smallish side for regression; regression remains mathematically possible but inferentially questionable. Second, these data violate at least one of the assumptional prerequisites for regression, the assumption of independence. Regression, and almost all statistical inferential techniques—that is, techniques that quantify uncertainty and thus allow an analyst to reach conclusions based on how likely the observed patterns are to have occurred strictly by chance—assume that observations are randomly selected and unrelated to each other, or *independent* of each other. Because these data are phase-level data, the multiple phases within a case are not independent of each other; they clearly relate to each other, they are sequential, and the factors in various phases vary in (non-random) ways determined by previous phases. What has happened before in earlier phases of the case clearly affects what happens in later phases of the case.

While we did not conduct any regressions, we did use a multivariate technique for which these data are appropriate—in fact, for which they were intended: qualitative comparative analysis. QCA was designed by sociologist Charles Ragin to assess configurations of case similarities and differences using simple logical rules.[6] Through the use of "truth tables," QCA provides a holistic approach to qualitative his-

[6] See Charles C. Ragin, *The Comparative Method: Moving Beyond Qualitative and Quantitative Strategies*, Berkeley, Calif.: University of California Press, 1987.

torical comparison by viewing cases in terms of combinations of binary (present or absent) factors.[7] Using computer algorithms first developed for the simplification of switching circuits, researchers are able to compare a large number of cases as configurations, many more than they could possibly "hold in their heads" using traditional case-oriented comparative methods. This case-based approach to analytic aggregation allows for the quantification of otherwise voluminous amounts of qualitative data. As such, it compels researchers to be explicit about outcomes of interest and proposed causal relations, including necessary or sufficient causes as well as conditional or contributing causes.

Qualitative comparative analysis relies on the application of Boolean algebra to a "truth table" in which selected factors are scored present or absent (1 or 0) for all selected cases.[8] The truth table has as many rows as there are logically possible combinations of values for the selected factors. For example, including four binary factors in the analysis would result in $2^4 = 2 \times 2 \times 2 \times 2 = 16$ rows of possible patterns. Rows are first reduced by removing patterns of factors that do not occur in the data—that is, any row that does not correspond to one or more actual cases. So, in a four-factor matrix, if no actual case had all four factors present, that row would be discarded. Boolean algebra then allows further reduction of the combinatorial matrix to expose simplified patterns of relationships and determines the prime implicants.

---

7 *Binary* indicates that a factor can take on only two values. In our case, that is *present* or *absent*, always represented by 1 or 0, respectively. A truth table, then, is a collection of rows of 1s and 0s that represent every pattern of the presence or absence of factors of interest that appear in the data.

8 Boolean algebra was developed in 1854 by George Boole. Boolean algebra differs from standard high school algebra in two ways. First, values are logical rather than numerical values. These are *true* or *false*, *present* or *absent*, and are represented as 1 or 0. Second, logical values dictate slightly different mathematical operations, obeying slightly different mathematical laws. Many readers will be familiar with Boolean search operators, such as *and*, *or*, or *not*, which can be used in some search engines. The application of Boolean algebra here has two implications: It requires us to structure our data with logical values (true/false or, in our case, present/absent), and it allows complex patterns of data to be reduced to the minimum set of factors necessary to determine a pattern, called *prime implicants*. See George Boole, *An Investigation of the Laws of Thought*, Amherst, N.Y.: Prometheus Books, [1854] 2003.

Prime implicants are the minimally sufficient patterns of factors that fully describe the pattern of outcomes of a set of cases. In these analyses, we used QCA to seek patterns of factors representing project hypotheses that did not just correlate strongly with BPC effectiveness but that also constituted prime implicants and perfectly discriminated the effective phases from the less effective.[9] A simple set of prime implicants can be very illuminating, separating factors or conditions that are just positive from those that are critical.

Qualitative Comparatives Analysis Results

Our initial QCA model used all 55 phases in which capacity building was a primary objective, and it considered all of the binary factors with strong correlations with binary outcomes as possible pattern contributors. This initial analysis failed. Although there were indeed prime implicants—that is, patterns of factors that would discriminate the more effective phases from the less effective—these prime implicants were not simple. Nearly a dozen factors were involved, and they took on an unworkable variety of patterns of presence and absence. No simple combination of factors was always present or always absent in the most effective of the full 55 phases. This was not too surprising; 55 is a fairly large number of phases, and we know that BPC is complicated and rife with nuance, especially when we include phases in which relationship building was a primary objective.

Considering only the 40 phases in which relationship building was *not* a primary objective yielded slightly simpler prime implicants. Eight factors are required, but all 40 phases can be effectively separated into effective or less effective (successfully classified) without using any of the effectiveness factors to do the sorting. Table 5.3 presents the prime implicants and lists the number of phases classified by each implicant. Factors that classify more phases are more primary; those classifying a small number of phases are catching exceptional or dis-

---

[9] For an example of the application of QCA to historical case data and further explication of the method, see Christopher Paul, Colin P. Clarke, and Beth Grill, *Victory Has a Thousand Fathers: Sources of Success in Counterinsurgency*, Santa Monica, Calif.: RAND Corporation, MG-964-OSD, 2010.

Table 5.3
Selected Prime Implicants and Number of Phases Classified, Phases in Which Relationship Building Was Not a Primary Objective

Prime Implicant	Phases Classified (out of 40)
Effective BPC always occurred in phases in which • (1) the PN was in the top half of global GDP, (2) it invested substantially in the capability itself, *and* (3) it did not have low absorptive capacity	18
Effective BPC always occurred in phases in which • (4) BPC included a sustainment component and both of the following: – (5) either more than $55 million from the United States *or* (1) the PN was in the top half of global GDP – (6) Consistent funding/delivery of BPC *or* (2) the PN made a substantial contribution to developing/sustaining the capacity *or* (7) U.S. and PN interests in the region substantially aligned	16
Effective BPC always occurred in phases in which • (5) the United States spent at least $55 million, (8) the PN's World Bank Governance Indicator percentile rank was not in the bottom third, *and* either – (1) the PN was in the top half of global GDP, *or* – (3) PN absorptive capacity was not low *and* (7) U.S. and PN interests in region substantially aligned	17
Effective BPC also occurred in the phase in which • (3) partner absorptive capacity was low, (2) the PN did not make a substantial investment in the capability being developed, (6) funding and delivery of BPC were consistent, *and* either – (5) the United States spent more than $55 million, *or* – (1) the PN was in the top half of global GDP	1, but it is not classified by any of the other prime implicants

NOTE: Factors are numbered in parentheses to highlight differences and duplication.

tinctive phases. Classification totals do not add up to the total number of phases because some phases are successfully classified by multiple prime implicant pathways.

While these prime implicants are somewhat complex, they feature some unsurprising factors repeatedly and prominently. Specifically, they identify wealthy or well-governed partners (PN in the top half of global GDPs, PN not in the bottom third of World Bank Governance Indicator percentile ranks, PN not having low absorptive capacity), committed partners (investing substantially in the capability being developed, interests aligned with those of the United States), and significant investment on the part of the United States (BPC included a sustainment component, U.S. BPC investment at least $55 million during the phase).

Eight factors mixing and matching in complex ways still do not amount to simple prime implicants. Seeking greater clarity and simplicity, we applied QCA to still smaller subsamples. Taking the 40 phases in which relationship building was not a primary objective and omitting phases before 9/11 (since H4c received strong support) leaves 24 phases. There are quite a few different sets of prime implicants that can discriminate among these 24 phases, and some of these sets are both simple and interesting. Table 5.4 presents selected prime implicants that are under U.S. control (but that are still prime implicants; that is, the factor patterns listed completely classify the phases as more effective or less effective). Just three factors are required to classify all 24 phases.

These 24 phases can also be classified completely by factors that reflect characteristics of the PN only. Table 5.5 presents such prime implicants, again requiring only three factors to classify the 24 phases.

Taken together, the various QCA models considered confirm the supported hypotheses discussed earlier in this chapter. Nothing

Table 5.4
Selected Prime Implicants and Number of Phases Classified, Post-9/11 Phases in Which Relationship Building Was Not a Primary Objective (U.S.-controlled factors only)

Prime Implicant	Phases Classified (of 24)
Effective BPC always occurred in phases in which • (1) U.S. spending in the phase was greater than $55 million *and* (2) BPC efforts built a capability that unambiguously aligned with PN objectives	23
Effective BPC always occurred in phases in which • (3) Funding was relatively consistent from year to year	18

NOTE: Factors are numbered in parentheses to highlight differences and duplication.

Table 5.5
Selected Prime Implicants and Number of Phases Classified, Post-9/11 Phases in Which Relationship Building Was Not a Primary Objective (factors characterizing partner only)

Prime Implicant	Phases Classified (of 24)
Effective BPC always occurred in phases in which • (1) PN had a moderate or higher Human Development Index and (2) PN *and* U.S. interests predominantly aligned	23
Effective BPC always occurred in phases in which • (3) PN was in the top half of global GDP *and* (2) PN and U.S. interests predominantly aligned	22

NOTE: Factors are numbered in parentheses to highlight differences and duplication.

revealed in the multivariate analyses calls into question any of the bivariate tests of the hypotheses.

Narrative Observations

The 29 case narratives are very rich and detailed, and they provide a number of interesting insights that extend beyond the project hypotheses. While greater detail is in the narratives themselves, here, we briefly summarize four such insights that are supported across the narratives.

BPC takes time.

Many of the cases demonstrate considerable lags between the beginning of BPC and any discernable capacity development. Many cases also include long foundation-building periods in which the United States and the PN establish working relationships, find shared interests, build mutual trust, or do other kinds of groundwork necessary for actual capacity building to begin.

BPC in Colombia, for example, had to overcome an initial U.S. fixation on counternarcotics over counterinsurgency (instead of both) throughout the 1990s, as well as governance issues that led to a punitive funding decrement in 1996 and 1997. After the turn of the century, when BPC was broadened to include both counternarcotics and counterinsurgency, and once the Colombians were convinced that the United States was genuine in its desire to help, the BPC process led to substantial gains.

Context extends beyond the partner to include its regional neighbors.

Many of the project hypotheses address aspects of the partner: its security status, its interests, the health of its economy, its governance, its motivation for and support of BPC activities. While the case narratives confirm these factors as important, several narratives also suggest the importance of the broader context, including regional neighbors. Neighbors appear to be important in at least two specific ways. First, they are competitors for security (and, thus, BPC) attention. If another country is significantly involved with a partner's security situation or security forces, it can constrain the space available for the United States to conduct BPC. Second, neighbors provide an external reference point against which a PN can compare the BPC involvement it receives. "Keeping up with the Joneses" is alive and well in the BPC neighborhood. Even if a partner receives quite generous BPC funding or attention relative to its own absorptive capacity and security needs, if a regional neighbor is receiving more (in absolute dollar terms, in terms of specific equipment, or in any other terms that can be explicitly compared), it may make that comparison and be dissatisfied. This can strain the relationship between the United States and the PN, which can run counter to broader foreign policy goals or have a modest negative impact on capacity building.

Focused BPC is less dependent on contextual factors.

A wide range of contextual factors can make BPC more difficult (see the hypothesis test results earlier in the chapter for examples). However, the narratives suggest that in challenging contexts, BPC can still be successful if it is narrowly focused. BPC efforts that seek to build capacity for a relatively small formation, a small number of elite forces, or a niche capability are easier in general, and easier to separate from the disruptions that contextual factors might cause. Further, such modest focused successes can provide a foundation for more ambitious subsequent efforts.

However, while focused efforts are easier to execute in the face of adversity, insisting on a narrow focus can backfire. For example, in several narratives (such as Colombia) early U.S. BPC efforts for a partner were confined exclusively to counternarcotics while the PN faced a wide and more dynamic range of security challenges. Insisting on too narrow a focus can impede BPC effectiveness in at least three ways: (1) by causing relationship friction between the United States and the PN over the disconnect, (2) by causing the PN to give less attention to the BPC effort while it focuses on the broader problem, (3) by causing capacity built to be (inefficiently) repurposed from the intended focus to meet the broader threat.

You can't want it more than they do.

The narratives more than confirm the project hypotheses that address PN motivation. In the narratives, effectiveness is seriously constrained when the United States seeks to build capacity in an area of limited interest to the partner, or when the partner's commitment to the effort (in either the national government or the military) is low.

CHAPTER SIX

Conclusions and Recommendations

Conclusions

This research confirmed that effectiveness in BPC is, in large part, a product of the BPC inputs (funding and activities) and the context for those inputs (predominantly, characteristics or behaviors of the partner, but also the broader security context). The bulk of our findings are based on hypotheses about inputs or context, and, thus, our conclusions follow these two general themes.

Matching matters: BPC is most effective when U.S. objectives align with PN objectives and when BPC efforts align with the partner's baseline capabilities and absorptive capacity.

This single prominent observation inspired the central metaphor of this report: Find the right ladder, find the right rung. The historical cases show that BPC is effective when the capacity being built meets the interests of both the partner country and the United States (the right ladder) and when the BPC activities are a good match for the partner's baseline capability in that area and its capacity to absorb new materiel, training, and so on (the right rung).

Context matters: Certain characteristics or features of PNs make BPC more likely to be effective.

Specifically, the following properties are associated with greater effectiveness in BPC, historically:

- PN invests its own funds to support or sustain capacity

- PN has sufficient absorptive capacity
- PN has high governance indicators
- PN has a strong economy
- PN shares security interests with the United States.

Broad interest alignment was shown to be a particularly powerful contextual predictor by the qualitative comparative analysis.

Independent of PN context, there are several factors wholly under the control of the United States that correlate strongly with BPC effectiveness.

These factors, which are strongly endorsed by our analyses, are as follows:

- spending more money on BPC or undertaking more BPC initiatives
- consistency in both the funding and implementation of these initiatives
- matching BPC efforts with PN objective and absorptive capacity
- including a sustainment component in the initiatives.

The more you spend, the more effective you are.

Several identified constraints can reduce the effectiveness of increased spending and effort, and the benefit from increased spending is not linear (it follows a curve of diminishing returns). However, the basic fact remains: More spending correlates strongly with increased effectiveness. That said, *where relationship building is a primary objective, capacity outcomes may not correlate well with expenditures/efforts.* Unsurprisingly, when BPC resources are being used to "buy friends," the actual capacity built is not always a primary concern. Even when capacity building is also a primary objective, the correlation between expenditure and capacity built is weaker. This does not in any way suggest that desired outcomes were not reached; in most cases, where relationship building was the primary objective, the relationship or level of access either improved or was maintained.

Post-9/11 BPC efforts have been much more effective.

At the juncture between inputs and context, as it relates to both the global context and how the United States viewed and conducted BPC, this study found that post-9/11 BPC was much more effective than the efforts of the preceding era. This suggests that future historical work should consider treating 9/11 as a historical "left bound."

Testing project hypotheses for each of five different BPC objectives individually led us to conclude that characteristics that correlate with BPC effectiveness do so across specific BPC objectives. However, *low absorptive capacity was not found to inhibit ministerial capacity building*. The narrative results also suggest that *ministerial capacity building can lead to increases in PN absorptive capacity for other BPC areas.*

Chapter Five concluded with some observations from the case narratives that bear repeating:

- BPC takes time.
- Context extends beyond the partner to include its regional neighbors.
- Focused BPC is less dependent on contextual factors.
- You can't want it more than they do.

Many of the project hypotheses were supported by strong correlations, but none of those correlations were perfect: No single factor perfectly explains all BPC outcomes. BPC is complex, but there are some clear best practices for those conducting BPC, clear best traits for desirable partners, and clear best practices for partners receiving BPC. QCA shows that when all three are followed, effectiveness is all but ensured. That is, *if BPC is consistently funded and delivered, supported and sustained, well matched to partner capabilities and interests, and shared with a partner that supports the effort and is healthy economically and in terms of governance, prospects for effective BPC are very good.* The QCA results also suggest that BPC can still be effective when only some practices are followed or certain conditions are present. BPC done well, done consistently, and matched to partner absorptive capacities and interests can be effective even when the partner is not particularly robust in any dimension at the outset. Find the right ladder, find the right rung.

Recommendations

These conclusions suggest several clear recommendations for DoD both for future planning and execution of BPC and for investments in the creation and maintenance of BPC capabilities.

Where possible, choose partners that have or can adopt the attributes, characteristics, or behaviors that are associated with effective BPC.

We recognize that foreign policy imperatives or the nature or location of a threat will sometimes dictate or force priorities when choosing partner nations; however, when there is flexibility in partners and priorities, choose partners that have or will adopt contextual factors associated with BPC effectiveness. Specifically, give preference to countries

- that are willing to invest their own funds to support or sustain capacity
- that have sufficient absorptive capacity
- that have high governance indicators
- that have strong and healthy economies
- whose broad strategic interests predominantly align with U.S. interests in the region.

Regardless of the partner or context, choose BPC goals and activities to correspond with what the partner wants or needs and what it is capable of absorbing.

As noted, strategic imperatives can compel partnerships in which the partner lacks some of the attributes that were prioritized in the first recommendation. Whether working with ideal partners or suboptimal partners, prospects for effective BPC increase dramatically when specific BPC objectives align with specific partner interests (independent of broader alignment with U.S. interests), and if the specific BPC activities conducted are well matched to partner baseline capabilities and absorptive capacity. As the metaphor repeated throughout the report suggests, find the right ladder, find the right rung!

For continued BPC effectiveness, the United States should build or maintain capabilities in the following ways.

- *Plan BPC activities to match both U.S. and PN needs and objectives.* Finding the intersection between U.S. and PN objectives is easy in some instances and quite tricky in others—especially when the intersection of interests is limited or nuanced. Planning and coordinating BPC activities to meet U.S. and PN objectives (and thus maximize prospects for success, both in BPC and in broader policy) is nontrivial. Such capabilities are and remain essential.
- *Identify baseline PN absorptive capacity and match BPC activities to what the partner can absorb.* Matching activities to PN baseline capabilities and absorptive capacity is also critical. DoD must have the capability to conduct needs assessments, identify baseline partner capabilities, and determine PN forces' initial levels of absorptive capacity (including equipment, organizational characteristics, readiness, the extent of existing training, technological sophistication, education, language abilities, and doctrine) to be able to optimally plan and match BPC activities to PN needs.
- *Build ministerial capacity and otherwise develop absorptive capacity.* Ministerial capacity (the capability of a partner's ministry of defense or ministry of interior to plan for and manage the partner's military and security forces) is foundational to other forms of capacity. Further, we found that ministerial capacity can be improved even when PN absorptive capacity is generally low and that ministerial capacity building can, itself, improve a partner's absorptive capacity, thus enabling future capacity building in other areas. Such capabilities should be central to the future BPC toolbox.
- *Consider sustainment capabilities in BPC planning.* Sustainment considerations are highly correlated with long-term effectiveness in the 29 cases discussed here. Whether it involves building a separate logistics capability or funding stream or expanding existing programs and capabilities to facilitate sustainment, effective BPC requires sustainment.

Opportunities for Further Research

This research project was ambitious and quite broad in scope. While it provides a strong initial empirical foundation for resource planning for BPC (29 country cases over 20 years of recent history), more can still be learned about this complicated mission area. Here, we present several possible suggestions for future research.

Conducting BPC with Suboptimal Partners

This report recommends that, where possible, the United States should choose partners with certain characteristics. We recognize, however, that such choices are not always possible: Strategic imperatives can compel BPC with countries that lack the identified characteristics; they are suboptimal partners. While our findings note several factors that correlate with BPC success that are independent of partner context, it stands to reason that there are further practices, capabilities, or features of BPC that increase the prospects for success when working with suboptimal partners. A more detailed examination of cases selected specifically to identify best practices under less-than-ideal circumstances should provide planning and capability development guidance for such unavoidable contingencies.

Deeper Analysis of a Few Case Studies to Gain Greater Insight into the Characteristics of Effective BPC Efforts

Because of the long period covered, the extent and complexity of BPC in general, and practical resource limits, the 29 case studies supporting these analyses are of limited depth. This is, in part, why we lost the preliminary hypotheses listed in Box 3.1 in Chapter Three. Deeper examination of a smaller number of cases could provide greater detail and a more nuanced understanding of the effectiveness of practices and activities at a lower level of granularity. In addition to getting more "into the weeds" of specific BPC activities, these detailed case studies would seek to exhaustively identify all U.S. BPC efforts conducted in the case country during the target period. (In contrast, the 29 cases here focus only on the most significant BPC activities.) Data collection would involve interviews at the COCOMs and the service components at the delivery level, and it might also involve interviews with PN personnel. Specific cases could be selected based on criteria identified in this study.

Greater Focus on a Specific Class of BPC Objective

Case selection for this study focused on BPC priority as revealed through funding level. To the extent that certain BPC objectives (perhaps ministerial capacity building or maritime security) or activity areas (joint exercises, training, equipment provision or sales) can be identified as likely future priorities, a study could focus on those objectives, activities, or areas, selecting cases to best illuminate the topic of interest. Depending on the area of interest and the level of analysis at which related policy questions are aimed, such a study could either consider a moderate number of cases at the same level of depth as our study or focus on a smaller number of cases at much greater depth.

A Focus on Efficiency

Our study found many strong correlates for BPC effectiveness, but an examination of what makes BPC more efficient—that is, which approaches or goals maximize effectiveness while minimizing costs—was beyond the scope of this research. In a fiscally constrained environment, improving efficiency is essential, and research on BPC efficiency an obvious next step. Future studies could build upon the foundation laid here to inform further data collection and analyses with this focus.

Lessons Learned from the BPC Efforts of Others

The United States is not the only country that conducts BPC. Several high-level U.S. partners, such as France and the United Kingdom, conduct significant security cooperation efforts, as do some multinational bodies, such as the United Nations. Any of these study opportunities could be adapted to incorporate careful consideration of the BPC activities of other countries and what has or has not worked well for them.

APPENDIX

Subordinate Factors for the Modified DSART BPC Objectives

As discussed in Chapter Two, our evaluation of the five capacity-related BPC objectives in each phase of each case relied on a number of subordinate factors. This appendix lists these subordinate factors.

Subordinate Factors for BPC Objective Category 1: Internal Security

- Ability to train military forces for counterterrorism, counterinsurgency, or counternarcotics operations
- Ability to carry out surveillance, reconnaissance, and intelligence operations
- Ability to maintain security throughout the country, including protection of critical infrastructure; ability to prevent terrorist/insurgent attacks
- Sufficient ministerial capacity to plan and integrate strategy and operations
- Ability to combat corruption
- Ability to police, prosecute, and incarcerate drug traffickers, terrorists, and insurgents
- Ability to deploy rapid and mobile reaction capabilities
- Logistics for, and maintenance and sustainment of, these capabilities
- Ability to establish drug eradication and interdiction programs (conditional)

Subordinate Factors for BPC Objective Category 2: Conventional Forces

- Ability to train military forces for conventional and regional security operations
- Ability to maintain an effective defensive posture
- Ability to carry out surveillance, reconnaissance, and intelligence operations
- Ability to conduct conventional military operations
- Logistics for, and maintenance and sustainment of, these capabilities

Subordinate Factors for BPC Objective Category 3: Specialty Forces

- Ability to collect and analyze intelligence on terrorists, narcotics traffickers, and pirates (conditional)
- Ability to train civilians and military forces in counternarcotics and the policing, prosecution, and incarceration of drug traffickers and pirates or in conducting counterterrorism/special operations or peacekeeping/peace enforcement
- Ability to protect and repair critical infrastructure and restore or provide basic government services
- Ability to deploy for and conduct operations outside own borders (e.g., for counterpiracy, counterterrorism, counternarcotics, peacekeeping/peace enforcement, humanitarian assistance, or other stability operations)
- Logistics for, and maintenance and sustainment of, these capabilities

Subordinate Factors for BPC Objective Category 4: Ministerial Capacity

- Degree of civilian control of the military and defense apparatus
- Systems of defense planning and financial management
- Professionalism of military forces in terms of education and training
- Military personnel policies capable of recruiting and retaining high-quality soldiers and officers
- Effective organizations for logistics, maintenance, and sustainment
- Security forces that carry out their functions in accordance with the principles of accountability and respect for human rights
- Ability to combat corruption

Subordinate Factors for BPC Objective Category 5: Border Security

- Ability to carry out surveillance, reconnaissance, and intelligence operations
- Ability to interdict illicit materials being smuggled in or out of the country through land and water
- Ability to combat corruption
- Ability to coordinate with neighboring states on border and maritime security issues
- Ability to train military forces in border and maritime security
- Ability to respond to incidents at sea, including boarding and retaking pirated vessels (conditional)
- Ability to disrupt and dismantle trafficking and smuggling networks
- Ability to prosecute and incarcerate pirates, traffickers, and smugglers
- Ability to conduct counterpiracy or countertrafficking training and exercises
- Logistics for, and maintenance and sustainment of, these capabilities

References

Calfee, Sharif, Joseph Lee, Peter Crandall, and Young Rock An, "Enhancing Interagency Cooperation," *Joint Force Quarterly*, No. 61, 2nd Quarter 2011, pp. 102–107.

Defense Security Cooperation Agency, "Frequently Asked Questions (FAQs)," web page, last updated August 15, 2012. As of September 24, 2012: http://www.dsca.mil/PressReleases/faq.htm

———, *Historical Facts Book*, Washington, D.C., various years. Most recent edition, as of September 30, 2010: http://www.dsca.mil/programs/biz-ops/factsbook/default.htm

Moroney, Jennifer D. P., Beth Grill, Joe Hogler, Lianne Kennedy-Boudali, and Christopher Paul, *How Successful Are U.S. Efforts to Build Capacity in Developing Countries? A Framework to Assess the Global Train and Equip "1206" Program*, Santa Monica, Calif.: RAND Corporation, TR-1121-OSD, 2011. As of September 24, 2012: http://www.rand.org/pubs/technical_reports/TR1121.html

Moroney, Jennifer D. P., Adam Grissom, and Jefferson P. Marquis, *A Capabilities-Based Strategy for Army Security Cooperation*, Santa Monica, Calif.: RAND Corporation, MG-563-A, 2007. As of September 24, 2012: http://www.rand.org/pubs/monographs/MG563.html

Moroney, Jennifer D. P., and Joe Hogler, with Benjamin Bahney, Kim Cragin, David R. Howell, Charlotte Lynch, and S. Rebecca Zimmerman, *Building Partner Capacity to Combat Weapons of Mass Destruction*, Santa Monica, Calif.: RAND Corporation, MG-783-DTRA, 2009. As of September 24, 2012: http://www.rand.org/pubs/monographs/MG783.html

Moroney, Jennifer D. P., Joe Hogler, Lianne Kennedy-Boudali, and Stephanie Pezard, *Integrating the Full Range of Security Cooperation Programs into Air Force Planning: An Analytic Primer*, Santa Monica, Calif.: RAND Corporation, TR-974-AF, 2011. As of September 24, 2012: http://www.rand.org/pubs/technical_reports/TR974.html

Moroney, Jennifer D. P., Joe Hogler, Jefferson P. Marquis, Christopher Paul, John E. Peters, and Beth Grill, *Developing an Assessment Framework for U.S. Air Force Building Partnerships Programs*, Santa Monica, Calif.: RAND Corporation, MG-868-AF, 2010. As of September 24, 2012: http://www.rand.org/pubs/monographs/MG868.html

Office of the President of the United States, *National Security Strategy*, Washington, D.C., May 2010. As of September 24, 2012: http://www.whitehouse.gov/sites/default/files/rss_viewer/national_security_strategy.pdf

Paul, Christopher, Colin P. Clarke, and Beth Grill, *Victory Has a Thousand Fathers: Sources of Success in Counterinsurgency*, Santa Monica, Calif.: RAND Corporation, MG-964-OSD, 2010. As of September 24, 2012: http://www.rand.org/pubs/monographs/MG964.html

Paul, Christopher, Russell W. Glenn, Beth Grill, Megan P. McKernan, Barbara Raymond, Matt Stafford, and Horacio R. Trujillo, "Identifying Urban Flashpoints: A Delphi Derived Model for Scoring Cities' Vulnerability to Large Scale Unrest," *Studies in Conflict and Terrorism*, Vol. 31, No. 11, 2008, pp. 1032–1051.

Ragin, Charles C., *The Comparative Method: Moving Beyond Qualitative and Quantitative Strategies*, Berkeley, Calif.: University of California Press, 1987.

Schaefer, Agnes Gereben, Lynn E. Davis, Ely Ratner, Molly Dunigan, Jeremiah Goulka, Heather Peterson, and K. Jack Riley, *Developing a Defense Sector Assessment Rating Tool*, Santa Monica, Calif.: RAND Corporation, TR-864-OSD, 2010. As of September 24, 2012: http://www.rand.org/pubs/technical_reports/TR864.html

Serafino, Nina N., *The Global Peace Operations Initiative: Background and Issues for Congress*, Washington, D.C.: Congressional Research Service, RL32773, June 11, 2009.

———, *Security Assistance Reform: "Section 1206," Background and Issues for Congress*, Washington, D.C.: Congressional Research Service, RS22855, January 13, 2012.

U.S. Agency for International Development, *U.S. Overseas Loans and Grants, Obligations, and Loan Authorizations* (*Greenbook*), Washington, D.C., various years.

U.S. Agency for International Development, U.S. Department of Defense, and U.S. Department of State, *Security Sector Reform*, Washington, D.C., February 2009. As of September 24, 2012: http://www.state.gov/documents/organization/115810.pdf

U.S. Code, Title 10, "Armed Forces," Section 168, "Military-to-Military Contacts and Comparable Activities."

U.S. Code, Title 10, "Armed Forces," Section 1051, "Multilateral, Bilateral, or Regional Cooperation Programs: Payment of Personnel Expenses."

U.S. Code, Title 22, "Foreign Relations and Intercourse," Chapter 39, "Arms Export Control."

U.S. Code, Title 22, "Foreign Relations and Intercourse," Section 2305, "National Security Assistance Strategy."

U.S. Department of Defense, *Quadrennial Defense Review Report*, Washington, D.C., February 6, 2006a. As of September 24, 2012: http://www.defense.gov/qdr/report/report20060203.pdf

———, *Building Partnership Capacity: QDR Execution Roadmap*, Washington, D.C., May 22, 2006b. As of September 24, 2012: http://www.ndu.edu/itea/storage/790/BPC%20Roadmap.pdf

———, *Security Assistance Management Manual (SAMM)*, Washington, D.C., DoD 5105.38-M, April 30, 2012. As of September 24, 2012: http://www.dsca.mil/SAMM

U.S. Department of Defense, Office of the Inspector General, *Joint Warfighting and Readiness: DoD Execution of the Warsaw Initiative Program*, Arlington, Va., D-2005-085, July 1, 2005. As of September 24, 2012: http://oai.dtic.mil/oai/oai?verb=getRecord&metadataPrefix=html&identifier=ADA435334

U.S. Department of State, Bureau of Political-Military Affairs, *Colombia: Security Assistance*, Washington, D.C., October 17, 2008. As of September 24, 2012: http://www.state.gov/t/pm/64493.htm

U.S. Department of State and U.S. Department of Defense, *Foreign Military Training and DoD Engagement Activities of Interest*, fiscal years 1999–2009, Washington, D.C., 2000–2009.